THE MARCH TO MONTERREY

The Diary of Lieutenant Rankin Dilworth, U.S. Army

To Louise with my best regards
Joseph E Chance

THE MARCH TO MONTERREY

The Diary of Lieutenant Rankin Dilworth, U.S. Army

A Narrative of Troop Movements and Observations
on Daily Life with
General Zachary Taylor's Army
During the Invasion of Mexico

Edited by
Lawrence R. Clayton and Joseph E. Chance

Illustrations by Wil Martin

Texas
Western
Press

The University of Texas at El Paso

Southwestern Studies No. 102

1996

The University of Texas at El Paso
El Paso, Texas 79968-0633

First Edition
Library of Congress Catalog No. 95-061096
ISBN 0-87404-198-8

Texas Western Press books are printed on acid-free paper, meeting the guidelines for permanence and durability of the Committee on Production Guidelines for Book Longevity of the Council on Library Resources.

Wil Martin is an Associate Professor of Art at The University of Texas-Pan American in Edinburg. His drawings have been exhibited in numerous one-person shows throughout the United States and in Mexico. He has received major awards in national and international juried exhibitions.

This book is dedicated to the memory of
Calvin L. Chance, Jr.,
who was my dear brother.

Joseph E. Chance

This book is also dedicated to my wife,
Sonja Irwin Clayton,
my constant helper in these and other matters.

Lawrence Clayton

CONTENTS

Acknowledgments ix

Introduction xi

The Diary

April 1

May 3

June 23

July 39

August 45

September 57

Conclusion 69

Notes 73

Bibliography 115

Acknowledgments

A great many people have been helpful in bringing this long lost piece of work to its present state. Principal, of course, are Charles Passel and his wife, Alda. Mrs. Passel insisted that Charles bring the diary to Dr. Clayton to see if it were worthy of attention.

Others deserving acknowledgment include Susan P. Walker, archivist of the U. S. Military Academy at West Point; the St. Louis Chamber of Commerce's Tourist Division; Dr. James Ivey, director of the Hardin-Simmons University Theatre Department; Dr. Kenneth Jacobs and Dr. B. W. Aston of the HSU History Department; Dr. Edward Hughes of the HSU Geology Department; Alice Specht, director of HSU Libraries; Dr. Murl Sickbert of the HSU Library staff; and Dr. Jerry D. Thompson of Laredo State University.

For their technical expertise, the authors wish to further acknowledge the aid of Kevin Young of IMAX Theatre, San Antonio, Texas; Jon Harrison of Texas State Technical College, Harlingen, Texas; Tom Fort of the Hidalgo County Historical Museum, Edinburg, Texas; and Gerard Mittelstaedt of the McAllen Memorial Library, McAllen, Texas.

Particular thanks go to Mrs. Charlene Archer and Mrs. Eva Martínez, without whose help the manuscript would not have been transcribed and continuously corrected. Special appreciation goes to Howard B. Passell, brother of Charles.

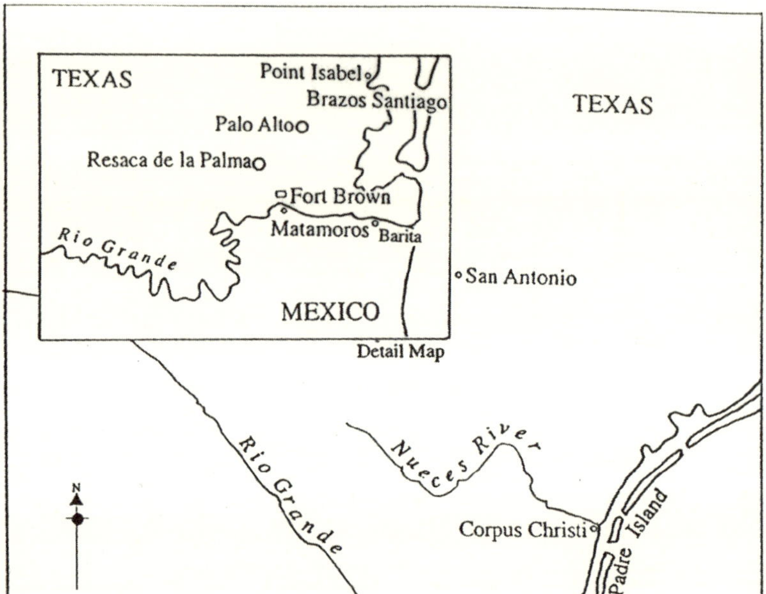

TEXAS
Point Isabel
Brazos Santiago
Palo Alto
Resaca de la Palma
Fort Brown
Matamoros
Barita
Rio Grande
MEXICO
Detail Map
TEXAS
San Antonio
Nueces River
Rio Grande
Corpus Christi
Padre Island
N
Camargo
Mier
Cerralvo
Rio de San Juan
Monterrey
Saltillo
Reynosa
Point Isabel
Brazos Island
Fort Brown
Matamoros
Detail Area
MEXICO
Gulf Of Mexico
0 50 100 150 200 250 kilometers
0 50 100 150 miles

INTRODUCTION

Family records reveal that Rankin Dilworth was born on February 19, 1822, in Mills Grove, Ohio, to Abram and Martha Judkins Dilworth. Nothing is known of his early life, but correspondence from young Dilworth, only seventeen years of age, to officials of the United States Military Academy forcefully expressed a desire to enter that institution. His mother, who by this time signed her name as Martha J. D. Evans, had apparently been widowed, remarried, and was a single parent. The family must have been of modest means, as Dilworth described his own situation in a letter to the secretary of war written in 1840 saying that he must "depend upon [his] own resources." Dilworth was accepted as a cadet, and his mother certified her consent in a letter dated April 28, 1840. He proudly entered the academy at West Point, New York, from Floydsville, Belmont County, Ohio, on July 1, 1840, four months past his eighteenth birthday.

The Plebe or Fourth Class of 1841, of which Rankin Dilworth was a member, contained thirty cadets. From these ranks came men who would later serve with him in northern Mexico and some who would later lead Union and Confederate troops in the American Civil War. The conduct roll for 1841 lists Rankin Dilworth with forty-one demerits; the same page lists Cadet Ulysses S. Grant of the Third Class with sixty-seven, both cadets falling far short of the two hundred demerits required for a dismissal recommendation by the Academic Board. Demerits were awarded for offenses that were graded into seven categories; the most serious were the offenses of introducing spirituous liquors into the barracks and disobedience of the orders of a military superior (both eight demerits). However, for the same offense, an upperclassman would receive more demerits than a plebe. Dilworth received a maximum of ninety-six demerits his third year, and was ranked moderately high in conduct over his four-year stay at West Point.[1] His grades placed him as thirteenth of twenty-five in his graduating class of 1844.

Six years after admission to the United States Military Academy, Rankin Dilworth chose to record the first entry in the diary while stationed with the 1st Infantry at Jefferson Barracks, outside St. Louis, Missouri. His last and final entry, dated September 19, 1846, found him with Gen. Zachary Taylor's army poised for an attack on the heavily fortified eastern side of Monterrey. In this attack, on September 21, 1846, young Lieutenant Dilworth was struck down and mortally wounded by a Mexican cannonball.

The editors of this diary hope that their efforts are a fitting memorial for Rankin Dilworth and all his comrades that were slain before the walls of Monterrey, and serve as a reminder to our readers, who we hope might pause for a moment to think of the sacrifices made by many of our fine young men and women who so proudly serve their country.

The life of Rankin Dilworth is remembered today only in the cold statistics of the official records (Register of Graduates and Former Cadets at West Point) which tersely note:

1218 Rankin Dilworth
B-OH: Inf: Mortally wded Monterrey: D-27 Sept 46 2LT a-24.

These records would remain as his only earthly testament, had it not been for Charles Passel, a descendant of Rankin Dilworth. Mr. Passel had found Dilworth's diary in materials belonging to his mother, Mrs. Cornelia Beakley Passel. Her mother, Abigail P. Dilworth Jones, was Rankin Dilworth's sister, and had received his personal effects after his death. Her name plate is affixed inside the cover of the diary.

The small diary in which Dilworth composed his record measures six by eight inches, a handy size to carry on a military campaign. It is of sturdy construction, coming from a time in our history when quality writing materials and binding were more important than today. The paper is approximately twenty pound weight by modern standards, and shows no water marks. The spine, once covered with leather, is now protected with blue adhesive tape, as the threads used to sew the gatherings are weak with age. The stiff boards are marbled and in remarkably good condition considering age. The corners of the volume are dog-eared and rubbed, and some pages are mottled by occasional discoloration, mute evidence of its daily exposure to the weather and the rough treatment expected in the military camps of southern Texas and northern Mexico.

The little diary also served as a composition book for Lieutenant Dilworth. Although the threads have parted on the first gathering of the book, an essay written in the same careful hand and entitled "On the Rise and Fall of Nations" is found in the front portion, and on the last page of that gathering and the first of the other is a lyric-like passage praising the beauty and trials of life. These two pages are not included in this book.

Some of the pages in the first gathering have been torn out, perhaps for use as writing materials by the author, or by some unknown censor who read the material after Dilworth's death. No diary text materials are missing; the diary begins on the third leaf of the second gathering and proceeds through two additional gatherings and part of a third for a total of ninety-four consecutive pages.

The text is mostly written in a very graceful hand, evidently composed on a table or a desk. However, some entries show a somewhat cramped style indicative of field entries transcribed in poor light or with the book braced on the author's leg in some unstable resting position. The characters in the earlier portions of the diary are in a very fine line in black ink. Later a blunter pen is used, but the ink color remains the same. The fine script returns from time to time, indicating the possibility of Dilworth's using an amanuensis. Little emendation was made by the author, but a few sentences are left unfinished.

Rankin Dilworth's diary documents the life and times of a young American officer summoned to south Texas to implement the war policy of the James K. Polk administration. The dispute between the United States and Mexico, although of a more general nature, focused on the admission of Texas to the Union, and specifically to possession of the so-called Nueces

Strip. The Republic of Mexico claimed the Nueces River as the southern boundary of Texas, while the United States asserted the Rio Grande as Texas's southern boundary. Possession of the Nueces Strip became the tangible issue used to initiate the war.

In June 1945 Brevet Brig. Gen. Zachary Taylor was ordered to move his "army of observation" into the disputed area in order to protect American claims to ownership. Taylor's initial buildup took place north of the present Corpus Christi, near the Nueces River at a camp-site well chosen to assert American interests in the Nueces Strip without unduly exciting Mexican authorities.

The winter of 1845 passed without diplomatic resolution of the boundary dispute between the United States and Mexico, despite several American efforts. President Polk, whose patience was exhausted by the Mexican government's cold shoulder, ordered the movement of Taylor's army into the disputed Nueces Strip in March 1846. President Polk hoped that this aggressive action would pressure Mexico to the bargaining table. But he had critically misjudged the Mexican Government's resolve to retain possession of its northern borders. Mexican national honor, gravely insulted by the loss of Texas, was now aroused to the brink of war. At a time in their history in which government overthrow occurred almost as frequently as the change of season, no Mexican president who wished to retain his office could now dare to hint of any negotiations with the Americans.

After a march overland from his winter camp near Corpus Christi, General Taylor settled his army on the Rio Grande opposite Matamoros without Mexican armed opposition. the American camp had to be supplied by provisions from ships off-loaded at Point Isabel, about twenty-five miles northeast of Matamoros on the Texas coast. Supplies were then hauled by wagons over land in their final leg of the journey to the camp on the Rio Grande.

The Mexican Army which garrisoned Matamoros almost immediately began to erect earthen works across the river designed to place the American camp in a crossfire. In response to this threat, General Taylor ordered the construction of a single large earthen fortification. Originally named Fort Texas, it was to become known as Fort Brown, in honor of its first commander Maj. Jacob Brown, who was later killed while defending this fortress from Mexican attack. Fort Brown was the nucleus around which the city of Brownsville would later be built.

A short period of uneasy peace descended on both sides of the river as both armies awaited further orders from their political leaders. American soldiers daily lined the banks of the river to view their Mexican counterparts across the river. Tops on every young soldier's list of favorite customs was the practice of daily nude bathing by women in the afternoon. In the balmy evenings, the pleasing sounds of music filtered across the river from Mexican regimental bands playing romantic arias from operas.

The first armed clash of the war occurred on April 25, 1846, near Rancho de Carricitos on the north bank of the Rio Grande. Mexican cavalry forces of Anastasio Torrejón ambushed a patrol of United States Dragoons led by Seth Thornton, capturing Thornton and most of his troopers. In his official report to Washington on this clash, Taylor wrote that "hostilities may now be considered as commenced...." Gen. Mariano Arista, under orders from the Mexican government, had begun offensive actions to remove Taylor's army from the Rio Grande. Torrejón's cavalry was the vanguard of a Mexican force of infantry, cavalry, and artillery that was to cross the Rio Grande from both above and below Taylor's camp. General Arista planned to place Taylor's outnumbered forces in the jaws of a trap by cutting off all supplies from Point Isabel. Arista began crossing his infantry below Matamoros at Longoreno by April 30, but was delayed in this movement, giving the American army precious time to escape. Taylor's forces with a train of supply wagons left the Rio Grande camp on May 1, and by a forced march toward Point Isabel managed to out distance the pursuing Mexican infantry. Maj. Jacob Brown and about five hundred defenders were left behind to garrison Fort Texas. By May 3 the booming of cannons at Fort Texas, as reported by Dilworth, commenced to be heard by the American soldiers as far away as Point Isabel. The Mexican army had commenced an attack on that garrison.

Three days were spent by Taylor's men strengthening the defenses of Point Isabel against possible Mexican attack, but finally on May 7 the American army turned its face toward the Rio Grande again and marched to relieve the siege on Fort Texas.

On the road between Point Isabel and Fort Texas, Taylor's army delivered two stinging defeats to the Mexican forces that blocked their way—at Palo Alto on May 8, and at Resaca de la Palma on May 9. The battle at Palo Alto clearly demonstrated the superiority of the new highly mobile American artillery, while the battle at Resaca de la Palma was highlighted by hand-to-hand combat with saber and bayonet. The defeat of the Mexicans on May 9 was complete, and a disorganized and routed Mexican force was driven back across the Rio Grande to Matamoros. Lieutenant Dilworth saw his first action a few days later in the capture of the Mexican village of Barita.

From Barita, Taylor had hoped to launch a flanking operation to capture Matamoros, but this effort was to prove unnecessary. American forces crossed the Rio Grande on May 18, and General Taylor accepted the surrender of Matamoros without opposition. The remnants of the once proud Mexican army retreated from Matamoros on a disastrous march to the west through an arid land marked with dry water holes. Their final destination was Monterrey.

President Polk, who had signed a declaration of war against Mexico on May 13, felt that the best American strategy for rapid victory over Mexico was to "conquer a peace." Polk ordered General Taylor to commence offensive operations that would lead to the capture of northeastern Mexico. For the first time in our history, American soldiers would be engaged in a foreign country on a war of conquest.

The military strategy for this region was dictated by geography. The Sierra Madre Oriental, a rugged range of mountains extending into Mexico from the west at the Big Bend and curving east to Tampico, effectively walled off the northeastern section from the remainder of the Republic. In 1846, only one major connection existed; the ancient trade route that passed through the mountains between Saltillo and Monterrey. The capture of Monterrey by American arms would effectively seal the fate of northeastern Mexico. However, between Matamoros and Monterrey, a distance of almost two hundred miles, the country was a semi-arid desert that had neither the water nor the food to support a large body of men and horses. General

Arista's disastrous overland march with his army from Matamoros to Monterrey had convinced General Taylor that Monterrey must be approached from some other route.

The route of advance to Monterrey was finally dictated by the availability of supplies and water. It was decided that troops and supplies were to be moved up the Rio Grande by steamboats to the village of Camargo, about a hundred miles from Matamoros overland. Camargo is situated on the right bank of the Rio San Juan, about four miles from its confluence with the Rio Grande. From this site, using wagons and burros to transport supplies, the American army was to march over land southwest to Monterrey, following well-watered routes near the Rio San Juan and the Rio Alamo. The little village of Cargo became a major depot for American supplies shipped from the mouth of the Rio Grande on that marvel of mid-nineteenth century American technology, the high-pressure, sidewheel, shallow draft steamboat. The Quartermaster Department, as early as June 1846, had agents traveling the Mississippi River to purchase or charter for federal service the needed steamboats. Thus began an extensive riverboat traffic on the Rio Grande.

General Taylor's immediate problems were then to find more soldiers to fill the thin ranks of a peace-time American army that had been decimated for the past generation by Congressional cost-cutting. President Polk solved this problem by an act that requisitioned from the several states a quota of volunteer soldiers for federal service of one year or until the end of the war. State enlistment stations were swamped with glory-seeking recruits, and thousands of disappointed men had to be turned away as quotas were rapidly filled. By July 1846, white tents marking the camps of volunteer regiments were seen at Brazos

Island, and along the north bank of the Rio Grande from its mouth up to Matamoros. In fact, many more volunteer soldiers were recruited for service than could possibly be used in the campaign against Monterrey. Many of these volunteers spent their year of federal enlistment in Rio Grande camps and not a few sickened and died from unsanitary conditions there. The poet's admonition that "the paths of glory lead but to the grave" was tragically fulfilled as many a young man was destined to fill an unmarked soldier's grave far away from home on the banks of the Rio Grande.

The American expeditionary force, numbering but six thousand volunteer troops and regular soldiers, was assembled at Camargo and ready to advance on Monterrey by August 19, 1846. The army marched southwest toward Monterrey by divisions, with that of Gen. William Worth as the vanguard. Dilworth's diary graphically reports on the assembly of Taylor's army at Camargo and the resulting overland march. After a period of rest and consolidation a Cerralvo, the army completed the march and was camped on the outskirts of Monterrey by September 19. American engineering and topographical officers sent to examine the newly constructed defenses of Monterrey returned that evening with very sobering reports.

The city had recently been well fortified by Mexican military engineers to withstand attack. Military structures lined both sides of the roads leading into Monterrey from the north and the west. These defenses were specifically designed to place the roads into Monterrey under an intense crossfire of artillery shot and shell. Looming to the north of the city stood La Citadela, a bastioned fortress of thirty guns that dominated the principal roads leading into Monterrey from the north. To the east of this imposing structure stood two earthworks: La Tenería, with three guns, and El Rincón del Diablo with like armaments. The roads to Monterrey from Marin and Monclova passed between la Citadela and the two earthworks. The road from Marin was further blocked at the head of La Puríssima Bridge inside the city by a fortification manned by artillery and infantry. The eastern approaches to the city were protected by imposing mountains and the Santa Catarina River. The road leading into Monterrey from Saltillo, to the west of the city, was dominated by the two hills which it passed between, Loma Independencia and Loma Federación. On the heights of the former hill stood a fortress armed with artillery, and on the latter stood La Obispada, an abandoned bishop's palace, fortified by artillery and infantry.

The garrison of Monterrey, commanded by Gen. Pedro de Ampudia, consisted of more than ten thousand soldiers, many of which were professionals belonging to veteran regiments. The streets of Monterrey, through which an invading army would be expected to pass, had been converted to death traps. The houses that lined the streets on both sides were stone two-story buildings whose walls were drilled for gun ports, and whose flat roofs were sandbagged for sniper emplacements. The principal street intersections were barricaded, and field artillery emplacements blocked the passage of traffic in four directions.

Against these mighty defensive works, an American army of about six thousand men with a feeble complement of three pieces of siege artillery advanced to the attack. On the night of September 19, General Taylor and his staff developed a daring plan to capture the city. Against the more numerous Mexican defenders, the American army would divide into two attacking forces. One, consisting of General Worth's division, was to circle the city from the west, seal off the Saltillo road, and advance into the city from that direction. With the remainder of the Americans, General Taylor would create a diversion on the eastern side of Monterrey to keep General Ampudia from committing his reserve forces to the western side of the city against Worth's division. General Taylor's diversionary attack was to probe Mexican defenses on the east side of the city for weakness, and hopefully to gain a foothold into the city from that direction. On September 20 Worth moved his forces into position, and the next morning the dual assault by American soldiers on Monterrey began.

On the western side of Monterrey, General Worth's division successfully captured the fortresses on Loma Independencia and Loma Federación with a minimum of casualties. But Taylor's attack on the heavily fortified eastern side of the city met with a stiff resistance, resulting in many American casualties.

The first wave of attackers, regulars led by Col. John Garland, braved the deadly crossfire of cannons from La Tenería and the Citadel to enter the forbidding city streets on the eastern side. The fields of tall sugar cane on the east side of the city had not been burned by the Mexicans and offered the Americans a refuge from cannon fire. But the Americans became lost in the tall cane and veered from their intended route to enter the city on a street too far west of their destination. From loopholes in the stone buildings that lined the streets and from atop the roofs, Mexican muskets poured death and destruction into the ranks of the American attackers. Rankin Dilworth was struck down in the crossfire from the fortresses before he could reach the streets of eastern Monterrey.

Many of the young American officers leading the attack, such as Dilworth, had no actual combat experience and did not allow their troops to take cover, ordering them to advance through these corridors of death. The chain of command became confused, and men ordered to retreat from the city were met by men ordered to advance into the city as their reinforcements. Before this day was over, many American troops would have been ordered to run the gauntlet of crossfire between the Citadel and the Tenería/Rincón del Diablo fortresses on as many as six trips. The chronicler of the First Tennessee Regiment, denoted as the "Bloody First" for its long list of casualties taken on the eastern side of Monterrey, wrote that, "Short after shot crashed through our ranks or enfiladed our line, strewed its pathway with mangled bodies, shattered limbs, and headless trunks; but unheeding all, on we rushed, over dead and wounded...." It was on this attack that young Lieutenant Rankin Dilworth was mortally wounded, living until September 27, long enough to probably receive confirmation of the great American victory.

The diary, while primarily a military chronicle, also reveals the cultural values of a mid-nineteenth-century young man. The girl he left behind, referred to as "E." or Emily, was the object of his thoughts and letters he sent home. But as with most romantically inclined young men of his time who visited Mexico, he was intrigued with the beauty of Mexican women. On the streets of Matamoros, when approaching a "very handsome Mexican young lady," he and his companion "raised our caps high to her paying that homage which beauty always claims." He describes another señorita as "by far the handsomest female that I had seen since I parted with E. M. M. She was very beautiful...walked like a queen..." and possessed "a pair of lips that could not be surpassed." Dilworth was a lover of all forms of beauty, and his descriptions of the flora growing along the river are characteristic of a keen and sensitive observer.

His attitude toward the prospects of battle may offer some possible explanation for his early death. Rankin Dilworth may have thrown his life away before the defenses of Monterrey in some act of naive chivalry or bravery, as dictated by the romantic image of war prevalent in the literature and culture of the time. He described the "cheering prospects of a campaign," and commenting upon the dangerous mission he was sent on to capture Reynosa, wrote, "...it was particularly agreeable to overhear them saying that we were marching to our own funerals."

The reader should note that the modern spelling of the principal city of northern Mexico is "Monterrey." The name was spelled "Monterey" during Dilworth's time.

In transcribing the diary, the editors rendered the most accurate and readable version we could. The original longhand entries were decipherable, within reason, a few places called for "editorial intrusion." We made these choices as wisely as possible based on the letters apparently present and contextual suggestion. Standardized spellings were used to aid the reader. Where words were apparently needed but not present, we inserted them in brackets to facilitate understanding. If the meaning of a sentence fragment seemed clear, we allowed it to stand because of the diary format. Familiarity with the names of ships and officers in that area at this time aided greatly in some of the deciphering since content was of no assistance in these cases. This part of the work was indeed a labor of love, albeit a demanding and often frustrating one. Often solving the "mystery" of the true rendering of name brought the joy experienced by those assembling a puzzle.

Lawrence Clayton
Joseph E. Chance

December 10,1995

APRIL

April 28, 1846

Garnett[1] came down express with an order for companies of the command to proceed to Texas. I was at Major Walker's[2] at the time that the news came in. Terret[3] was there with his betrothed. I pitied them. They had to part, but as yet no one knew what companies were to go. In the afternoon, however, it was ascertained that companies C, E, and K were to go.[4] The officers of the command were Lieutenant Colonel Wilson,[5] Comander; Brevet Major,[6] Captains Miller,[7] Backus,[8] and La Motte;[9] Lieutenants Wood,[10] Barry,[11] Terret, Carpenter,[12] Plummer,[13] and Dilworth. Companies F and I were to be broken up and the privates transferred to the other companies. Their officers, Captain Jouett[14] and Lieutenants Mumford[15] and Masten,[16] were left behind to be sent on the recruiting service. The colonel[17] and the band were left.

On the twenty-sixth I had written a long letter to Emily and was taking it to the Post Office when the news came. I wrote on a small piece of paper "marching orders for Texas, April twenty-eighth R. D." and slipped it into the letter. The next day I wrote again letting her know that we were off. Nothing under heaven was done towards getting us off till after muster on the thirtieth.

April 30, 1846

After muster this day, at about eleven o'clock, Captain Jouett's black servant brought me a large bouquet with Miss Taylor's compliments saying that she had brought it all the way from the city. She came on horseback, a short time after Captain Jouett informed [me] that Miss Medosa [Taylor] and Miss Eliza Taylor were at his quarters. I spent the afternoon with them, and in the evening we all went to a polka party at Lieutenant Jenkin's.[18] We danced the polka for the last time at Jefferson Barracks.[19]

Miss Medosa and I walked out by the flag staff. The moon was shining very brightly. We spoke of our absent friends and of parting with those that were near.

MAY

May 1, 1846

I had all my baggage packed and directed to John F. Jones[1] at Vermont, Ill. and sent it to St. Louis. I rode up to the city with Miss Medosa Taylor. We went about one mile beyond to attend a May party. Mrs. Dean was there. I bid them goodbye and returned to the city. In Miss Medosa I had a sincere friend. In fact I know of none from whom I disliked parting so much as from the whole Taylor family.

During the day I bid farewell to all my friends. Partings are very affecting. I attended the theater in the evening to hear Mr. and Mrs. Keen's poor play.[2] Miss Sylvie, now Mrs. Russell, reminded me of E[mily]. M. M. She looked *very* handsome.

May 2, 1846

At five o'clock this day we marched out of Jefferson Barracks, where we had been since the twenty-fourth of September, 1845.

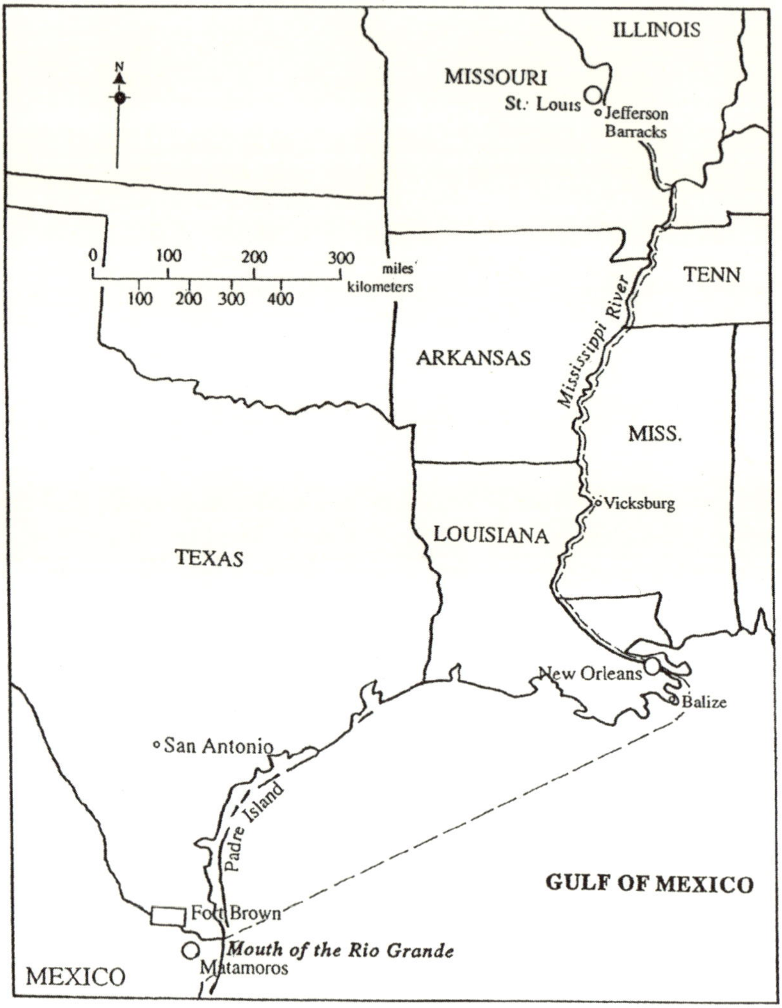
ILLINOIS
MISSOURI
St. Louis
Jefferson Barracks
0
100
200
300
miles
kilometers
100
200
300
400
TENN
Mississippi River
ARKANSAS
MISS.
Vicksburg
LOUISIANA
TEXAS
New Orleans
Balize
San Antonio
Padre Island
GULF OF MEXICO
Fort Brown
Mouth of the Rio Grande
Matamoros
MEXICO

We left many warm hearts that beat kindly towards us never to meet some of them again. The ladies accompanied us to the steamer, which was about one mile below. The boat left about dark. The moon was up, and it was about the same time in the evening and the moon was about as high in the heavens as when we left Prairie Du Chien[3] in September last. We left the shore amidst all the noise of the band, field music, and the loud cheers of the men.

May 3, 1846

Major Walker, Pay Master, was aboard for the purpose of paying the men. I was attached temporarily to K Company.

After leaving the mouth of the Ohio River, we frequently met flat boats whose crew would frequently salute us with "Heurra for Texas!" "Give them Hell!" Our mate rigged a flag using a broom for a staff, the broom being to sweep out the Mexicans.

May 6, 1846

At dark in the evening we rounded to at Vicksburg. The drums were beating, and our flag and broom at mast head. I was going on shore to get the last news when a gentleman come on board. The sentinel was about [to] stop [him] when he asked to see the commanding officer or officer of the day. I called to Wood when the stranger, a Mr. Hurst,[4] asked me if I had learned the last news. I replied that I was just going on shore for that purpose. He then told me that they had news from Texas of the twenty-seventh that on the twenty-fifth of April the Mexicans had cut off Captain Thornton's detachment of the 2nd Dragoons killing thirteen and taking all the others prisoners.[5]

Lieutenant Kane was killed,[6] Captain Thornton missing, Captain Hardee[7] and Lieutenant Mason[8] prisoners. General Taylor had made a call on the militia of Texas and the Southern states[9]. This was great news for us. Instead of remaining inactive at Matamoros, we now had the cheering prospect of a campaign. We left Vicksburg amidst the cheers of our own men and the inhabitants on shore.

Between this and New Orleans, the whole country seemed to be turning out. There were crowds of persons on the shore with flags up.

May 8, 1846

At evening we rounded to at New Orleans. The whole city was under arms. Never since the time when it was about to be attacked by the English has there been such an excitement. Parties were marching up and down the streets with the drums going with a vengeance. In the evening I called on General Gaines[10] and his lady at the St. Charles Hotel,[11] took a small supper at a restaurant, and returned to boat. As we landed a number of ladies were standing on the guard of one of the boats at the landing waved their handkerchiefs to us. Terret told me not to return it, for we knew not who they were. I told him that I never let a lady wave to me without returning it, so we had a glorious wave. The boat passed down and then returned and took its place behind the one on which the ladies above referred to were on board. I was on the hurricane deck[12] at the time with all the other officers. The ladies came out, and I could hear them saying, "There he is, there he is, the one with the white pants." The pilots came to me and said, "There are some ladies on board that boat who must be relatives of yours."

"No," I told him, "I never saw them before."

"What,"said he, "Are they making such a fuss about then?" So much for returning the courtesy of a lady.

May 9, 1846

We marched from the Hannibal[13] to the Galveston,[14] a sea steamer. I was left in command of K Company and could not get on shore but [a] short time. A Mr. Brano, brother-in-law to Lieutenant Thompson,[15] lst Dragoons, came on board and introduced himself and expressed his regret that we could not remain longer in the city, for he could make our time pass very agreeably, for which we thanked him and threatened to trouble him when we returned. At four o'clock we left the wharf and landed at the barracks to take on board two companies of Volunteers.

I went into the barracks and found Mrs. Dana's[16] quarters. Miss Kitty Sandford and Lieutenant Dobbins[17] were present. I thought that poor Mrs. Dana would have gone into fits. Her husband was in danger, and we were soon to be with them or die trying. The garrison was filled with citizen soldiers who formed a most perfect rabble, some drunk, others drilling, and quite a number trying to get out of the sally port.[18] I mentioned to Mrs. Dobbins that it must be very disagreeable to have such a crowd around them. She replied that it would be under any other circumstances, but these men are enrolled to rescue our husbands, who are surrounded by an enemy. When the first company of them came down, I felt as though I could have gone down to receive them myself. She gave me a letter to take to her husband with the injunction to deliver it if possible.

It was just one week from the time that we left Jefferson Barracks, and by moonlight the Volunteers marched on board. It was then found that we had no cartridges on board. The Quarter Master had depended on the Lieutenant Colonel, and the Lieutenant Colonel had depended on the Quarter Master. I was sent with twenty men for them, and then had to go down the river to a schooner to get a box of flints.

A report had reached the city that the sale of two Mexican steamers, which we had heard of sometime ago, was a mere ruse to get them out of port and that there were two privateers off the mouth of the river to cut us off. A vessel also brought in news that Captain Walker[19] of Texas with a company of volunteers had left Point Isabel and had all been cut off except the Captain and three men. Captain Walker had returned to the Point with these men and immediately applied for four more, determining to cut his way to General Taylor's Corps. For our protection on our voyage the Governor sent on board a twelve pounder.

There was a crowd of carriages full of ladies on the shore, and when we left, a national salute was fired.

May 10, 1846

I waked up in the morning and looked out of the window of my stateroom to see where we were. We were just passing the Balize.[20] The broad, blue sea was before us. The steamship New York[21] came alongside in a few moments. They had left Point Isabel on the sixth. We could not understand all that was said but heard that the noise of cannon[22] was heard at Isabel on the day that they left.

Several sails came in sight but passed at a distance. We saw the smoke of a steamer in the south and, after many surmises as to her character, discovered her to be the Alabama[23] from Galveston. Saw a brig of war but could not make her out.

We all expected to be seasick, but the Gulf was so very smooth, and we spent a very pleasant day. We were out of sight of land the whole of it. Saw this day the sun rise and set at sea for the first time in my life.

A small bird that must have been blown from land followed us for some time, so wearied that it could scarcely fly. After being frightened away several times, it at length lit on the guard and remained a fellow passenger for some time.

May 11, 1846

Had a clear day but at night an awful storm. I was very sick, as well as many others. Terret in particular was sick all the time. He declared that he did not enter the service to go to sea. My stateroom was too confined so that I confined myself to a sofa in the cabin. Terret was on another on the opposite side. The boat pitched and rolled at an awful rate. The lightning was very vivid, but there was such a roar of the sea that the accompanying thunder could not be heard. Terret called the Captain of the ship to him and said, "Captain, I am very, very sick indeed. Do you think that it will get any smoother soon?"

"No," he said, "It will get rougher and rougher."

"Oh Captain, this is a very rough sea now."

"Very smooth, very pleasant sea indeed."

In the midst of all this roar I was just falling to sleep when the cry ran through the ship of *"a man overboard."* There was never anything which sent such a chill of horror through me. It was impossible to save him, and we did not stop the boat. He was one of the Louisiana Volunteers,[24] and had the *mania potia.*[25] There had been a guard over him, but watching his opportunity, he sprang upon the guard and exclaimed "Goodbye boys" and sprang into the sea.

May 12, 1846

On account of the storm we did not arrive off Point Isabel[26] till the evening of the twelveth. The steamer Augusta[27] had just arrived with the artillery from the New Orleans Barracks. They had been out one week. The whole Gulf Squadron lay off the Brazos Santiago.[28] [Note inserted by Dilworth]: [I] saw a party of horsemen on Padre Island,[29] along the shore of which we had been coasting since daylight when St. Joseph's Island[30] was in sight. The Captain of the Galveston swore that they were Mexicans and that Point Isabel must have been taken. They proved to be Captain Price's Company of Texian Rangers.[31]

May 13, 1846

We disembarked by means of other steamers. But on account of the roughness of the sea, we did not get our baggage on shore till dark. General Taylor was at the Point. He had left in the morning but hearing that there were two thousand Mexicans between this point and Matamoros, he had returned. The Point presented all the wild excitement of a time of war. [Note inserted by Dilworth: I heard from a naval officer[32] of the battles of eighth and ninth.]

May 14, 1846

The day passed without anything being done except that we had orders to march early the next morning for Burrita,[33] a village in Mexico about nine miles from the mouth of the Rio Grande in a direct line, but fifteen miles by the river. It was the point at which all the Rancheros[34] had crossed who annoyed our army for some time before the battles of the eighth and ninth. There were three routes from Point Isabel [to] Burrita, the distance eighteen miles. The first was by land and struck the Rio Grande opposite Burrita. This road was good and dry. The second led directly to our point of destination [a] distance [of] seven miles but three miles of it was through a lagoon of three feet water. The third was by the way of Brazos Island and the mouth of the Rio Grande. The distance from Point Isabel to the mouth by this route was ten miles, and from there to Burrita eight [miles] making the route the same length as the first but with the addition of three water courses to cross. The navy was to cooperate with men and boats from the fleet off the mouth of the river.[35] The first two roads were objectionable on account of our having to cross the Rio Grande at Burrita, and as it was reported that the enemy was there, we would find it difficult to get over. The navy men also were to pass up the river, and it was necessary to have troops on shore for their protection. Consequently, we took the third route, although we would have sent our baggage by sea to the Rio Grande.

The remainder of the regiment of the Louisiana Volunteers arrived this day. Although the Lieutenant Colonel's order was that the Alabama and Louisiana Volunteers should form part of the expedition, he declined taking them along because he said that they were not here when the General published the order and of course could not have meant that they should be included. Colonel Walton[36] of the Volunteers ranked above him. When General Taylor issued the order, he knew that the Volunteers were hourly expected and delayed the hour of our march twenty-four hours longer than was necessary, no doubt to let them come up. Yet Lieutenant Colonel Wilson, for the miserable pride of commanding, left with a force of not 500 men to go into the enemy's country to an important point where it was possible that we would meet their army in force.

No baggage was to be taken along. Each officer and man had to carry three days' rations on their backs.

May 15, 1846

About eight o'clock this morning we marched out of our camp at Point Isabel. We could have got off much sooner, but the Quarter Master, Major Thomas,[37] did not for some reason best known to himself furnish us with wagons to transport our baggage to the landing. While cleaning up the camp one our men found a "Tarantula,"[38] a species of spider that would cover several inches in circumference and whose bite is worse than that of a rattlesnake.

We went on board at nine o'clock and landed on Brazos Island about four miles below the Point. We marched across to the beach and waited an hour or two for the Lieutenant Colonel and the Louisiana Volunteers, during which time I took a sea bath. It was glorious. The breakers were superior to those at Cape May or Rockaway.

About one o'clock we resumed our march. Our route lay directly along the beach near the water. We passed over many very handsome marine shells, but we were already too much loaded to pick any up. Every officer had his provisions on his back. At three o'clock we came to the Boca Chica[39] where we had to cross [to] the mainland. A scow had been sent from Point Isabel to ferry us over, but the shore was so shoal that we had to wade some distance on each side before we could get to the boat. Terrett came up while we were waiting for the scow and said, "Dilworth, do you want to see how to get fresh water? I can show you in a moment," and with his sword he immediately commenced an excavation in the sand. When he obtained water, it was, as Captain Lamotte observed, a little more salty than in the sea.[40]

About dark we arrived at the mouth of the Rio Grande[41] and encamped without tents, cloaks, or blankets and but little to eat on a number of sandbanks at the mouth of the river. I slept on the top of a sandhill and slept very soundly till morning. At one time I waked up and saw something pass near my face. My first thought was of a Tarantula. I sprang up, but it [was] only a shadow. I have often been alarmed at shadows.

May 16, 1846

Two weeks ago we left Jefferson Barracks. Today was very warm, and in the afternoon we had a rain. It came on to us without any resistance. The relief found some watermelons growing on the plain, but they were not ripe. On the opposite shore there were several houses, but we could not get over to partake of their hospitality. There was no sign of any movement in the navy, and the sea was so high that the boat with our baggage could not get out of the Brazos Santiago; so we had to remain the whole of the day. The Lieutenant Colonel would not let us procure any meat on the Mexican shore, so we had nothing but hard bread and water of about ninety degrees temperature to subsist us. About sundown Hamilton[42] of our regiment came down from Boca Chica, where he had come in a small boat. He brought also to Captain Desha[43] of the Alabama Volunteers a bottle of brandy, which was a perfect Godsend. All the officers partook of it except the Lieutenant Colonel, who gave as a reason for not doing it that he wished to keep as cool as possible. A *"council of war"* was held, and it was determined to proceed to Burrita at all events, and our baggage was to be conveyed in wagons if the steamer Neva[44] could not get into the river. We spent another night on the sand.

May 17, 1846

We crossed into Mexico at twelve o'clock this day. The steamer Neva had already arrived in the mouth of the river. For forty hours we had anxiously watched for her, and every smoke that had been seen off Brazos had produced an exclamation of "Yonder comes the boat!"

Our line of march was as follows: First the advanced guard. At one hundred and fifty yards in their rear came the Alabama Volunteers under Captain Desha. One hundred yards in his rear was the lst. U. S. Infantry with Captain Stockton's Company[45] of Louisiana Volunteers on the left flank. Capt. Sabin's Company[46] of Tennessee Volunteers were 100 yards in our rear. Lastly came the rear guard. The first mile and a half was through mud and water one foot deep. About two miles from Burrita two horsemen were seen [in] front of us. The Lieutenant Colonel sent the Adjutant to meet them, but they set spur and returned at full speed to the village.

At one mile from it we came in full view of Burrita. It was a beautiful spot. On the north side of it flowed the Rio Grande. For a distance of one furlong from the bank there was a perfect plain; then the heights on which Burrita stood rose abruptly to a distance of 100 feet. To the south it sloped into another plain, and at a distance of one half of a mile was a large lagoon. The southern slope was covered with small tropical trees. A number of horsemen came out to meet us, and the Lieutenant Colonel told them that the inhabitants would be kindly treated. They returned to report accordingly. We marched through the village without music and encamped near an old barracks that had been occupied by Mexican soldiers two years ago during a rebellion. There was a delightful sea breeze, although the day had been one of the warmest I ever felt. Captain Miller took off his cap, and looking around on the number of señoritas, expressed his satisfaction to being stationed here during the remainder of the Mexican War. I had a very bad headache, and as my tent was pitched, I retired.

May 18, 1846

We commenced entrenchments, for all the inhabitants had declared that we would be attacked this night. This morning I called on some of the señoritas, but in the afternoon most of the families left for fear of an attack at night. A flag staff was erected at the end of the old barracks, and the command gave three loud cheers as the Stars and Stripes ascended to its top and floated for the first time over Mexican soil, which we could claim as our own.

Two hundred sailors and marines came up today in their boats bringing with them two cannonades which were placed on the salient toward Matamoros and together with the six pounder, which we already had, made a respectable armament to our little fort. The men worked all day in the trenches. I marched on as senior officer of the guard this evening. It was an all-important night. All of the command had been brought within the trenches and encamped opposite the points that they were to defend. The guard was sixty strong with half of them Volunteers. The latter were of more trouble than value. It was almost impossible to keep them awake.

Two picket guards one of six men [and a] sergeant were posted on the Matamoros road. The other of the same strength towards the mouth of the river. The navy had also a guard over their guns, but the rest of the sailors and marines were at their boats at the river. A light was seen in the southwest, and an old ship's quartermaster mounted the flag staff with a glass to make observation. He reported the light to be "from small fires which covered an area as large as our camp. There was evidently an encampment about eight miles off."[47] Their camp fires, however, ended in smoke.

It very often happens that persons to avoid danger throw themselves directly into it. So it was with our friends from the navy. They were encamped on the bank of the river thinking of no danger but from the Mexicans where at the same time nothing but an accident saved them from falling by our guns. They had orders in case of an attack to retreat into the fort, but neither the guard nor one of the companies guarding the works toward them was aware of it. After twelve o'clock at night I sent Lieutenant Dickenson[48] of the Alabama Volunteers, who was the junior officer of the guard, to visit the picket guard on the Matamoros road. He missed and went on some distance beyond. Returning, he came upon the picket, who challenged, but he did not answer. Seeing him coming from the direction of Matamoros, the Sergeant was about to fire when he saw that the Lieutenant had but four men with him and concluded to take the prisoners. Had a gun been fired, the alarm drum would have been beaten and the parapet manned. Our navy friends would have heard, and, in getting to a place of safety, would have been fired upon from the fort.

May 19, 1846

The report in camp today was that General Arista[49] had left Matamoros and that General Taylor had crossed the river. An express from that place came in at one o'clock and confirmed it. And [we] were glad when the U.S. got the east bank of the Rio Grande, for the Indians could not then come. Some of the families who had left the village from a fear of the enemy's attacking us returned.

May 20, 1846

K Company went two miles up the river and crossed over for wood. We cut it on the bank of the river in a chaparral which presented more the appearance of a flower garden than a woods. There were innumerable varieties of flowers of the handsomest kind. The sensitive plants grew in great quantities. There were several species of cactus. Among the more familiar plants were the asparagus, tomato, and watermelon.

At night we had a violent thunderstorm. The rain inundated everything. I reached my hand out of my bed and found a perfect torrent all around my bed. Some of the men in the neighboring tents were sounding.[50] I could hear one call out six feet large. Another finally sang out "No bottom."

May 21, 1846

General Smith with the Washington Regiment of Louisiana Volunteers arrived.[51] There were any number of mounted officers, and they all had spy glasses. General Desha remarked that they wished to see the enemy at a distance.

May 22, 1846

Colonel Mark's Regiment[52] of Louisiana Volunteers arrived, and the steamers Neva and Cincinnati.[53] General Desha and myself had a dashing ride over the vega[54] on a couple of Mexican ponies. Took my last lessons in Spanish from the young Mexican who had taken a great deal of trouble to teach me. He had furnished my tent with a table and chair and in return I gave him my looking glass and pitcher, which it was impossible to take along with me. His wife kissed her hand to me to express the highest degree of thanks.

May 23, 1846

We marched this morning for Matamoros [with] General Smith in Command. Colonel Marks was left with his regiment of Volunteers. The road frequently touched the river and was bounded on both sides with thick chaparral. The whole country was like a magnificent flower garden. The day was excessively warm. One of the Volunteers fell dead on the march. The rear guard buried him and left a small cross to mark his resting place. We marched fifteen miles and encamped at the point where Arista had crossed the Rio Grande[55] previous to the battles of the eighth and ninth. There were a number of Ranchos on the road, at one of which we halted and got some refreshments. I laid myself on a bed and was falling into a sound sleep when our Lieutenant Colonel came in and asked the General if he had not better move on with his battalion for the men were beginning to go to sleep. We accordingly had to march.

At our camping ground there was a señorita who was by far the handsomest female that I had seen since I parted with E[mily] M.M. She was very beautiful. She was dressed in a loose white dress and walked like a queen. One of my sleeve buttons came off, and she volunteered to sew it on. When she had finished it, she drew my arm towards her mouth. I modestly held back when I saw a pair of lips that could not be surpassed approaching my hand, but she only wanted to bite off the thread.

Some of the boats were here in which Arista crossed, and a small trench which he had thrown up to cover his crossing. The rancheras (farmers) who were here had been in the fight but only as spectators.[56] I was officer of the guard this night.

May 24, 1846

Reveille beat at two o'clock this morning. One of the General's aides was anxious to move. It soon commenced raining, however, and we could not get off till dawn. As we had no tents, we were quite wet. It made the road very bad. When we came to start, the guide was not to be found. One of the men who had been on express to Matamoros put us the advanced guard in the main road, but Lieutenant Colonel Wilson marched his battalion [on] the wrong road, which detained us an hour longer. At seven o'clock we came in sight of

Matamoros.[57] It presented a fine appearance at a distance. At eight the advanced guard halted at the suburbs of the city to give the column, which had been prolonged in the chaparral, time to close up. While [we] remained here, General Taylor and staff came out to meet us. There was very little to be seen that would remind us that we were in a captured city, which but a few days before had witnessed such stirring scenes. It was Sunday and scarcely a soul was to be seen until the noise of our drums brought them to the door. It reminded me of days long passed. I reflected as we marched down the streets with all the "pride and circumstance" of war that at that moment our far distant friends were quietly assembling around their altars and perhaps were offering up prayers for our welfare.

We proceeded directly to the ferry,[58] crossed over, and encamped in Texas. The whole army was encamped on the two sides of the river and presented an appearance of which no one can form an idea except those who [have] seen a like one. I met many of my friends and classmates whom I had not seen since I left West Point. Took dinner with Lieutenant Dana of the 7th Inf.[59] We had taken but a slight breakfast at three in the morning, and we showed him a fine specimen of an appetite.

May 25, 1846

Visited the city and saw some of the inhabitants. Took some glorious punches at the Tienda Canon [Canyon Store], with some of my long parted friends. The city is decidedly an unmilitary one. All the important buildings [are] barracks, especially around the plaza. It stands one half of a mile from the river with long avenues of China trees leading to it.

I saw Captain Morrison[60] of the 4th. The fatigue of the eighth and ninth and subsequently together with loss of Clara had completely broken him down. He said that Georgiana had written that he must show me a great deal of civility.

May 26, 1846

Took a walk in a garden near our camp. It had been a magnificent one. It had been regularly laid out in walks bordered with limes, oranges, lemons, pomegranates, and almost all tropical fruits and plants. A regiment of volunteers had bivouacked in the midst of it and had cut down the trees to make shelters. Immense numbers of pomegranate trees had been cut down with the fruit nearly ripe.

The mail from the U.S. had been lost[61] between [here] and Point Isabel. The express rider was seen on his way drunk. Captain Walker of the Texas Rangers has been out for it.

May 27, 1846

Captain W found the mail rider and afterwards the mail, but there was nothing for me. Has E forgotten me?

June 1, 1846

"When ... taken prisoner, he threw it [his colors] into the chapparal, where it was afterwards found."

JUNE

June 1, 1846

I went into the city today and saw amongst the others a young lieutenant of the Tampico Regiment.[1] He said that his Regiment [had] been cut to pieces but the colors were on their way to Washington. He drew a rough plan of the two battles. He said that when he found that they would be beaten, he took his colors and put them in his hat. When he was taken prisoner, he threw it into the chapparal, where it was afterwards found.

The natives are leaving. The report is that Antonio Canales[2] is between this [place] and Reynosa with his Rancheros and that General Arista has been reinforced by 5,000 men.

June 3, 1846

Visited the chapparal where the battle of the ninth was fought. All the interesting spots were pointed out by Captain

Walker of the Texas Rangers and by Captain Bliss,[3] Assistant Adjutant General. We saw the graves of Lieutenant Inge[4] and Cochrane,[5] and also two graves in which were buried 150 Mexicans.[6]

June 4, 1846

Received orders today to cross to the Mexican side of the Rio Grande on the evening of the fifth in order to take up our march on the next morning for Reynosa. Hope we will have a fight. At all events we will move from this land of fleas and bedbugs. Lieutenants Thomas[7] and Johnson[8] go along with a section of Bragg's Artillery,[9] also a company of Texas Rangers.[10] The Mexicans dread the Texians more than they do the devil,[11] and they have good reason for it, if all the reports that we hear are true.

Went into the city and saw a very handsome Mexican young lady walking on the Plaza with one of the dignitaries of the city, who appeared to be her father. She was elegantly dressed. Haller[12] of the 4th was with me. We raised our caps high to her paying that homage which beauty always claims. The rumor is confirmed that Canales is between this and Reynosa. Report gives him from 700 to 3,000 men, with artillery.

June 5, 1846

I went to the Post Office as a last hope of hearing from E. There was no mail. I sent her a paper with some flowers which I had picked up on the field of the ninth, from the spot where this Tampico Regiment was cut up.

At one o'clock we had everything in the wagons and marched for the lower ferry to cross and be ready to march early in the morning of the sixth. As we marched down the road, we passed the camp of the Washington Regiment of Louisiana Volunteers, the lst. U. S. Artillery, and the 7th Infantry. Their officers were all on the road to bid us goodbye and hoped that we would give it to them good: "Let us hear of your doing well Goodbye, God bless you."

Our company was the last to cross, being on the left. The other companies had been detained by transient persons crossing in the boats, but when it came to our turn, Captain Miller told me to march the company into the two boats that were there and let no others go on board. In the small boat Captain Crossman,[13] two Mexicans, [and an] artillery officer had placed themselves, and another was going into it. Captain M ordered him to halt. Captain Crossman said that he was his clerk. "I don't care a d—n whose clerk he is; I [have] been detained here for five hours by persons crossing as you are doing."

"But I wish him to go over."

"I can't help it—-neither he nor you can go."

"Capt. Miller, are you in earnest?"

"I am."

"I won't obey it."

"What sir! — Bring a guard! — Lieutenant Dilworth, march down the company."

I accordingly marched it down, and we took possession of both boats. The two Mexicans after talking for awhile went to another ferry. The artillery officers were perfectly furious, but it was of no avail.

There had been a great difficulty in getting the baggage wagons out of the boat and up the bank as the mules had to be taken out. I, however, got a rope and fastened it to the wagon and made the company take hold of it. "Now," said I, "yell and go ahead! A yell!" They sent up an awful shout, and the wagon went to the top of the bank in an instant.

Afterwards, I again went over the river with my servant. We returned in a few moments, but as the Mexicans who worked the boat were gone, it had to be pulled over by our own party. The boats are drawn across the river by a rope which extends from one shore to the other. Priana, the wagon master, and Ely, my servant, had hold on it. After we were about twenty yards from the shore, the rope gave a surge which threw them both into the river. Priana let go and swam on shore, but the rope raised Ely some fifteen feet in the air. The poor soul could not swim but held on like grim death. We called to him to move himself to a small rope that was near and let himself into the water. By that means he got safe to shore.

In the meantime, we were floating down the river with only a pole on board which would not touch the bottom. The boat was full of mules, and every time that we tried to use the pole, it caused a perfect stampede. It was a delightful moonlight, and we floated along as calmly and gently as though we were on a pleasure excursion. I wish I had been a poet.

At length some Mexicans swam out and caught our rope and pulled us up.

Returning on the other side, the Lieutenant Colonel put me on duty to receive the provisions as they were brought over, which kept me there till eleven o'clock. One boat with about 300 bushels of corn and twenty men sank after leaving the shore. Some of the men came near drowning.

June 6, 1846

About twelve o'clock at night we had a violent storm of wind, rain, and lightning. When I lay down I was very warm and had thrown back the wings of my tent to let the air in. At twelve o'clock I was wakened by their flapping. While I was fastening them, the wind caught the tent and down it came. I caught up my blankets to take them into Captain Miller's tent, but when I got out I saw that it also was down. I went back and taking the ridge pole raised the canvas in the center and coiling myself around slept soundly till reveille. When I wakened, it was still raining very hard.

At two o'clock [we] marched. Our friends came out to bid us goodbye, and it was peculiarly agreeable to overhear them saying that we were marching to our own funerals. They all believed that we would have a fight, and so did General Taylor. Many thought that the General was to blame for sending so small a force so far into the enemy's country. Two of General Smith's volunteer aids got permission to go along as "amateurs." They said that they did not wish to return without hearing a Mexican musket, and they thought that this would be their only chance.

The roads very bad. I had command of the rear guard and was wading through the mud when General Taylor, who had accompanied us a few miles, came past and said to me, "This is very heavy marching, Lieutenant Dilworth."

"Yes sir," said I, at the same time raising my feet with about ten pounds of mud attached to each.

We encamped about five miles from Matamoros, as there was no other camping ground within twenty miles. (Note inserted by Dilworth: So the guide said, but there was a much better [place] both for defense and water two miles further.) Some persons occasionally make blunders but others are constantly making them. Or more properly, they blunder when they do a thing as it should be. Our encampment tonight would do honor to the ones at Burrita and the mouth of the river. In case of an alarm, one half would have shot the other. The orders to the guard were to fire if any armed body approached without waiting to challenge. The sentinels were very far apart, and returning to my guard (I was officer of the guard) with a patrol, I came near being fired upon. Our camp was in the midst of the chapparal.

June 7, 1846

Had a very hot march and encamped seventeen miles from Matamoros. The natives say that Canales is this side of Reynosa with 1200 men and six pieces of artillery.

Saw about one o'clock this morning a most brilliant meteor.

We halted at ten o'clock A.M. and marched again at twelve. At two P.M. we encamped on the bank [of] a lagoon in a beautiful valley.

About ten at night I was standing at the door of my tent talking to some other officers on the probability of meeting the enemy on the morrow. "Yonder," said I, "they come now," as I saw in the moonlight a party of horsemen winding along the foot of the bank at the edge of the lagoon. We were at a loss to account for them. The sentinel challenged, and they halted so that we knew that they were friends. Captain Miller immediately remarked, "A countermand from General Taylor, by G—."

"Yes," said another, "General Scott has arrived at Matamoros and has sent for us just as we were going to have something to do." When the Sergeant of the Guard, however, brought them up, we found them to be a party of Mexican countrymen who had left Matamoros and were taken by our Ranger picket.

June 8, 1846

Reveille beat at three o'clock, and we marched at daylight. Our way for the first few miles lay through a delightful valley about one mile wide, bounded by chapparal which resounded with early songs of birds. The road made a curve which enabled us to see the whole column. Far in front the advanced guard of Texas Rangers, Infantry, followed by the Artillery. Looking to the rear the dim light of dawn showed our long wagon train "on their winding way." At twelve we halted to rest, having had no water for several miles. Temperature about 110 degrees. I walked into the village and made arrangements for a dinner at the house of a man who had lived in the U. S. He was very pleasantly situated, his "casa" being surrounded by fig, orange, lemon, and China trees. Captain Lamotte and Major Abercrombie took dinner with me. When we bid him "adios," the old Spaniard said, "Gentlemen, when you return, this is your house."

It was raining when we returned to camp, but we marched at three P.M. The roads were miserably bad, and when we encamped for the night I was more fatigued than I ever was before. We had marched and waded eighteen miles that day and as soon as my tent was pitched I lay down, but felt so tired that it was ten o'clock before I went to sleep.

June 9, 1846

Heard nothing of reveille but was wakened up by my servant telling me that breakfast was ready. It was still bright moonlight without any sign of day. I felt fatigued and sick but was determined not to get into a wagon. After a few hours, however, I felt quite well.

The Lieutenant Colonel was informed during the forenoon that a party of the enemy occupied a certain chapparal and were going to fire on us and retreat. At ten o'clock we approached the chapparal in question. Halted, and the captains were ordered to see that their companies were ready for action. The priming of the pieces was examined, the flints picked, and bayonets fixed. The column with heads erect and a firm step marched into the chapparal anxious and ready at any moment to meet the enemy. But they were doomed to be disappointed.

We marched about five miles without any water except such as was occasionally to be found in a mud hole in the road, which was very seldom. At twelve we halted for a rest on the side of a pond of hot water; and remained till two P.M. temperature 120 degrees. For eight miles then we had nothing but green stagnant water. But at night after the march of eighteen miles we encamped on the bank of a lagoon which it would do one's heart good to see. I took a delightful bath. Our men when in Iowa or Wisconsin Territories could march ten or twelve miles without [water], but here too or three miles is sufficient to exhaust them. I carried a gourd full of water[14] strapped to my back. Nature seems to have provided a gourd on purpose to carry water.————-[small sketch of gourd in diary] represents a section of it. A cork can be easily inserted in the neck and a strap put around the small part. They hold from one to two quarts and keep the water very cool and pure.

June 10, 1846

Marched at dawn and [at] eleven o'clock came in sight [of] Reynosa.[15] The column halted at three miles from it, and Captain Lamotte was sent forward to demand a surrender of the place. On his way to the city he met Lieutenant Thomas' black boy (who spoke Mexican and had taken the liberty to ride ahead of the column) returning at full speed *with his hair standing on end* from fright. The town is full of Mexicans, said he. "They have built two forts that are full of soldiers who are also standing around them in crowds." The forts proved to be two unfinished houses and the soldiers a number of poor, half-naked Mexican inhabitants.

The town had sent a deputation to General Taylor immediately after the occupation of Matamoros to surrender the place on terms,[16] and as General Canales was several leagues off, there would be no doubt of the surrender. Captain Lamotte received from the Alcalde[17] a Texan prisoner who had belonged to Captain Price's company of Rangers, and had a brother who is now in it. He had been a prisoner for six months.

We marched on to the hill on which Reynosa is situated without music and took quiet possession of the town. Our camp was pitched on the best position which we could find, but even that was not a good one. There was no water within a half mile; the wells in the town were all brackish. The hill was composed of limestone so that no defenses could be thrown up, and the rock was so near the surface of the ground that it was with difficulty that a tent could be pitched. A village was directly in our rear with stone houses whose walls were from three to six [feet thick] and might, for all we knew, be full of the enemy, for there was no search or examination made. The roads leading to the town were so numerous that Canales might have occupied it and poured down a fire upon us from walls that our artillery could not shake. The Lieutenant Colonel in the evening was asked if he would receive a communication from General Canales. He said that at any time would either receive the General himself or any communication that he might send. He was then told that at eight o'clock the next morning he would receive a letter from General Canales. This made us think that he was near, and again we had the excitement of an expected attack. I was officer of the guard, as I was at Burrita on the eventful night at that place. No enemy came.

June 11, 1846

At eight o'clock the Lieutenant Colonel received the promised communication. It amounted to but little. Stated that he would cut us off if we endeavored to advance farther, which he could easily do as he had the whole country at his command. But he could not do it on the eighth or ninth of May.

This evening we marched in and occupied the public square. The men were placed in the quarters around it, but the officers had to occupy their tents. The plaza was covered with sand, which came over us like a simoom.[18] We had five watermelons.

June 12, 1846

Received a report that Canales had left his camp, which was about eighteen miles from this place, with his whole command (400 men) and had gone towards Monterrey.

June 13, 1846

An American came in today from Monterrey. He says that General Arista and Ampudia[19] have both been ordered to Mexico. General Mejia[20] is in command of the army, which amounts to 2000 men. The Mexican army is one day's ride this side of Monterrey. Canales is sixty miles from this raising men and has 800 men. One of the companies is twenty miles from this.

I marched on as officer of the guard. I was out with a patrol to the picket guards at eleven P.M. and hearing some persons speaking in a field near at hand, I ordered the escort to halt and went forward alone with my sword under my coat. Instead, however, of showing fright, they pulled me a watermelon, which was eaten on the spot "by the light of the moon."

June 14, 1846

Sunday. The guard is stationed near the church, and I had a fine opportunity of seeing the inhabitants. Some of the females were very well dressed. In the church were two clarinets and a violin. I wonder if I will ever go to church again where I will hear the English language spoken.

As we had to march on as officers of the guard every three days, the Lieutenant Colonel was kind enough to send word by the officer of the day, that the officer of the guard might sleep in the day time. I accordingly went to Barry's tent, which was near the guard, and soon fell asleep. In my dreams I was once more in church in my own native land without a thought of camps or bivouacs, with smiling happy faces around me. Barry called out, "Wake up, Dilworth, the guard is turning out." In an instant I found myself on the hot sandy plaza of Reynosa, many, many miles from those I love.

Remarks

Surface of the Country

From the Gulf shore, eight miles to Burrita the country is low and level interspersed with salt marshes and lagoons. Some places there are bushes of low mesquite and the sensitive plants intermingled. The grass is thick and sharp. At Burrita it becomes more elevated and continues so, to about twenty miles below Reynosa. As we come up the river the timber is larger and the surface of the ground is more undulating. Reynosa stands upon a hill about fifty feet above the surrounding country. The hill is limestone (secondary) and, I think, metalliferous. I saw to confirm my suspicion some rude pigs of lead said to have been smeltered from ore found in this vicinity.

Trees and Plants

All the tropical trees and plants grow here. The most common tree is mesquite, which forms almost all of the chapparal. The live oak was seen some twenty miles below Reynosa. The Spanish moss, asparagus, and *palma christa* (castor oil bean) are natives. The latter grows twenty feet high. The variety and beauty of the flowers cannot be surpassed. Cotton grows from Burrita to Reynosa, as well as the sugar cane. There is but little rain in the summers generally. Sometimes for seven months there is not a drop so that the grass is not as luxuriant as it would otherwise be. The farms generally appear well cultivated; that is, so far as they are planted. Corn grows luxuriantly. The soil [near] Burrita is not so good as it is higher up the river, where it cannot be surpassed.

Houses

Most of the houses are built with but one story. The lower classes live in mud walled huts with thatched roofs and ground floors. In Matamoros there are several fine two story brick buildings. The upper stories are used for dwellings with stores in the basement, but [in] Reynosa the better houses are made of stone with flat roofs made of cement with gravel mixed amongst it. The church at Reynosa must have cost an immense amount of money. The walls are six feet thick with a parapet wall around the top.

The inhabitants present all shades from the pure Indian to the white person. Their intelligence is in the same scale. They are perfectly indolent. The climate produces the necessities of life with but little labor, so that they live from one day to another without regard to the future. It is for this reason that the country suffers such internal commotions. Anyone who possesses power can mould them to their will. Their soldiers were mere tools. Some of them fought well. The officers were mostly intelligent, many of them foreigners. Their artillery was well served.

Reynosa June 10th

Nothing occurred to vary the time except a few storms which blew down our tents and gave us a complete drenching. Our time was spent sleeping, eating watermelons, and visiting the inhabitants. On the eighteenth it was rumored that 500 Comanche Indians were near on the Texas side of the Rio Grande. They were robbing corn fields and taking some of the inhabitants.

At dark they rode down the bank and reconnoitered Reynosa and then crossed over. A party of Mexicans were sent by the Alcalde after them but returned the next day without having done anything. The Indians had crossed onto this side of the river, and we afterwards learned that a great part of them [were] Mexicans.

No news from Matamoros. The natives say that [wagon] trains and steamboats [are] on the way, but afterwards we find that they belong to the 10,000 false rumors afloat. A gentlemen at this place received a letter from Monterey. It stated that some of the Mexican army had left Linares[21] and gone to Monterey to fortify. They had just heard that 300 U. S. troops had taken Reynosa.

June 21, 1846

No news. It is nearly one month since we have heard from the U.S. and fifteen [days] from Matamoros. In a few days we will be out of rations. An individual arrived today from Matamoros who says that a steamboat is on the way. This information can be relied on. I was wakened out of sleep this afternoon by hearing Barry say, "When did you leave Matamoros?" I went out and near my quarters was a company of Texas Rangers.[22] They were out and had been within eighty miles of Monterey reconnoitering. On Friday they had ridden all day without one drop of water. There is a steamboat in sight, *they say*. If it does not bring me a letter from E, I will————- [Dilworth's line is is incomplete.]

Steamboat arrived, and I received a long, *kind* letter from E and one from my mother.

June 22, 1846

Another boat arrived. Wrote a long letter today.

June 24, 1846

Was [with] Lieutenant Johns[23] [to]day. The Mexicans were galloping over town racing their horses, etc.[24] The Texas Rangers who came in on the twenty-first ran with them, but [the Mexican] ponies stood no chance with Texas horses. The Rangers were quartered in a cotton gin. And at dark, hearing a great noise, I looked out in that direction and saw them all on top of it dancing a war dance to the infinite amusement of the natives who were collected below.

June 25, 1846

Two Mexican officers, a Lieutenant and Ensign, were taken prisoners in our camp today. The Lieutenant Colonel was going to let them go on parole, but someone suggested that he was not the proper authority to give a parole and that persons taken without arms or uniforms were more of spies than prisoners of war. He accordingly confined them. I was Officer of the Guard and remained in the room with them. The Ensign during the night tossed and rolled about in his bed as though he was dreaming of hanging or shooting.

We have had constant rains for more than a week. There has never been such a wet "spell" known. The inhabitants say that it is on account of the approach of our army. If that should happen to be the cause, we certainly have the higher powers on our side for rain is the very thing.

June 29, 1846

Again on guard; nothing to vary the monotony of our life since the twenty-fifth. We look daily in vain for a boat. Don Ignatio Guerra is writing an address for the Fourth of July. He read it to Captain Lamotte and myself yesterday evening, but we understood but little of it. It commenced "Gentlemen of the North! Officers of the lst Regiment, U. S. Infantry." Both he and his son, a lieutenant, said that it was very good.

JULY

July 1, 1846

Canales is near Camargo, changing his residence daily. It has rained constantly for more than twelve days. Everything is mildewed in my tent. In fact, I begin to feel "mildewed" myself.

Today an accident occurred that would call forth pity from anyone. A soldier through gross stupidity shot another in the arm in their quarters. The ball tore his arm to pieces near the shoulder. It was amputated, but from the loss of blood he died in an hour after the accident. His name was Brown of G Company. He had a family in Pennsylvania, and had saved all his little pay for them, counting daily the length of time that he had to serve. He had but four months left of his enlistment.

Saw a Mexican from Matamoros who said that the steamboat Neva was at Mat[amoros]. He said [*Neva*] had returned to New Orleans and that the Frontier[1] in coming into the Rio

Grande was wrecked and one half the cargo was lost. The Mexican was going to Camargo to see about supplying the steamboats with coal,[2] which exists in abundance.

Spent a horrible night last night. It was with the greatest difficulty that I could keep awake. I would nod as I wrote. Had muster today and but little rain. The river is running over its banks.

Sent one of my letters to Matamoros by Señor Dr. Garcia. All of the lower town is under water, and river is still rising. The farmers are coming in with their families.

July 2, 1846

The river rose fourteen inches during the night. Have a fair day but very warm. Hope that we will have no more rain. There has not been such a freshet for ten years. It is impossible for a steamboat to get up now.

July 3, 1846

Lieutenant Hamilton, myself, and Don Jaspar Guerra were chosen managers of the ball for the evening of the fourth. The river is falling.

July 4, 1846

We have had no news from Matamoros since the twentieth. We looked hourly for a boat as long as the river was between its banks, but now we are as those without hope. I *see* that providence intends that we shall go no farther into the country. [Don Ignatio Guerra's] voice not permitting him to address a large crowd, he delegated his son to read it. Lieutenant Barry is sick today so that I am on guard tonight, with but two nights off.

The two Mexican prisoners wondered how we could stand it to go on every third night and do our other duties.

Our "speech" proved a failure. A number of invitations were sent round for the ball. I was very busy all day arranging the room. The inhabitants furnished chairs and benches. In the evening just before the company began to assemble, I went into a yard and took hold of a reed to fix one of the lights. The moment that my hand touched it, a scorpion stung me on the finger. I ran into the house, and a young señorita got some salt and applied it, and in an hour or two it ceased to pain me. The ladies began to arrive at 8 o'clock, dressed in their best. Some of them looked very well. We kept up the dance until three o'clock [on the] morning [of] the fifth.

July 7, 1846

Just before dark one of the principal men of this place died very suddenly. He had been in the ballroom but a few moments before he breathed his last. He was a relative of some of the best families, which kept them away.

We have had daily reports of steamboats being in sight, but none have come.

I this morning received a plate full of figs and pomegranates from a young lady. The figs were quite ripe and the first fresh ones that I ever ate. Captain McCullough[3] of the Texas Rangers came up today. Kendall[4] was with him. Kendall came into my tent where I was writing with my coat off. I immediately put it on, and as I pushed my arm into the sleeve, a scorpion stung me on the shoulder. I applied a little salt, and in a short time I did not feel any of the effects of it.

Captain McCullough reports the steamer with three companies of the 7th Infantry on the river enroute for Camargo.

July 8, 1846

The Aid[5] arrived at eleven o'clock, and the company encamped on the ground which we first occupied. The two Mexican officers were released from confinement on giving their parole. Lieutenant Colonel Wilson and Major Abercrombie were ordered to Matamoros on a court martial for the trial of Colonel Whistler,[6] Captain Thornton, and others. I received a letter from the Adjutant General stating that it was intended to transfer some Brevet Lieutenants into the new regiment of mounted riflemen and wishing to know if I would accept a transfer. But I have no wish to place myself voluntarily under two individuals who were cadets below me and not able to graduate.[7] I just begged leave to decline.

July 9, 1846

The report here is that eight more companies of the 7th are on their march, but by land. [They] had got into the water and were about to turn back. The three companies that are here are encamped on our old ground.

July 11, 1846

A steamer arrived with the companies above referred to. They had found it to be almost impossible to move on account of the overflow, and General Taylor had sent orders for them to proceed to the Rio Grande at the nearest point and wait for a steamer.

July 12, 1846

Another boat arrived with ammunition stores and left with the one that came yesterday for Camargo. The companies did not debark.

July 15, 1846

[The following note was written in but scratched through by Dilworth: "Steamer J. E. Roberts[8] arrived with three companies of the 5th on board."] The other three and Captain McCullough's Texas Rangers and the artillery section of Lieutenant Thomas have orders to march tomorrow at daylight for C[amargo].

The steamer J. E. Roberts arrived with three companies of the 5th on board enroute for Camargo.

July 16, 1846

Was very sick.

July 17, 1846

Still sick. Captain Chapman[9] of the 5th came into Reynosa today. His company was left by the steamer Roberts two miles above this. The boat was not able to get over a bank and part of the stores had to be taken out. Captain C was left to guard them.

July 19, 1846

Three other companies of the 5th came up under the command of Major Staniford.[10] I received no letters. General Taylor is made a full Major General. Colonels Twiggs[11] and Kearny[12] Brigadier Generals.

July 22, 1846

Another boat with two companies on board came up.

July 23, 1846

Gen[?] with two companies of his brigade [sentence incomplete]

AUGUST

August 5, 1846

One company of 2nd Artillery Captain O. Stewart[1] came up today and took up their quarters at Reynosa. Report says that we are going to march in a day or two. Almost all the regular army is above [i.e., at Camargo].

August 7, 1846

General Taylor and staff came up leaving orders for us to be ready to march tomorrow.

August 8, 1846

This day 500 men leave Matamoros for San Fernando.[2] At three P.M. we marched from Reynosa after a residence of two months. I bid farewell to the young ladies. Both sides of the street were lined with inhabitants, and "Adios, Señor, etc." was repeated on all sides. The country after we had marched two or three miles became quite rolling. From the top of one ridge we had delightful view. There was a broad valley, and the Rio Grande was to be seen winding its way through. There were three steamboats in sight. It became dark before we came to a camping ground, which was on the bank of a small arroyo, which we crossed after leaving two or three of the wagons fast in mud. There was a village on the opposite side called Rancho Maria.[3] Distance is eleven miles from Reynosa.

August 9, 1846

Reveille beat at three o'clock, and we had breakfast long before the moon had ceased to cast a very bright shadow. We had enough rain to drench us thoroughly. We marched a little after four. The reveille [was sounded?] on board a steamboat. The rain had made the roads horrible for marching. At seven o'clock we passed Reynosa Viejo,[4] a village containing about 200 persons. At nine we crossed arroyo and rested until one P.M. I marched on as Officer of the Guard and had to march in the rear to bring up stragglers. Very [many] fell out of ranks. They would keep up with the guard for a time and then fall out to the side of the road, declaring that it was impossible for them to go farther. Having no wagon with me, I was obliged to leave them. Towards dark they began to fire to ascertain where we were. A drum being beaten brought them to camp.

We encamped in beautiful valley on the margin of a swamp. On one side was a chaparral and the ground where the tents were pitched. It had just enough trees to make a good shade. I was very much fatigued and having to keep awake amused myself with writing the above at the guard station at eleven o'clock at night before tatoo. The scene was peculiarly wild and beautiful. But few tents were pitched, and campfires in the various groups revealed the men in the attitudes that painters give to bandits at their night fires.

At nine the moon rose and all was still and quiet. But for the rays falling on the scattered tents or the reflection from stacks of arms, all was like a vast solitude.

August 10, 1846

We marched at five o'clock. The road was very good. The same number of sick men in the rear as yesterday. Saw behind us the steamboat on which our heavy baggage was placed. Halted at nine-thirty o'clock and rested till two-thirty P.M. Got dinner at a Mexican house. Halted three miles from Camargo[5] for the night.

August 11, 1846

At seven o'clock this morning we marched into camp and took our place in the line. It was a magnificent camp on the bank of the San Juan.[6] The color line[7] extended one mile. On the right, next to Camargo was the

[Worth's Division][8]

Artillery battalion—eight companies, Commander Bvt. Lt. Col. Childs[9]
Capt. Duncan's[10] com Light Artillery
8th Infantry.—six companies, Capt. Shroner[11]
5th Infantry.—six companies, Major Staniford,[12] Commanding
lst Infantry.—four companies, Lieutenant Colonel Wilson

3rd Brigade
3rd Infantry.—six companies, Brevet. Major Lear[13]
4th Infantry [entry incomplete]

General Taylor's headquarters were in the town.

August 12, 1846

Began to police our grounds. News came in today that there were large forces at Monterey.

August 13, 1846

A circular order today that we must hold ourselves in readiness to March in eight days. Some companies of the 3rd and 4th Infantry came up by land this day with a train and Bragg's Battery of Artillery. The whole under the command of Lieutenant Colonel Garland.[14]

Volunteers arrive daily in steamboats. They are too aristocratic to march, although the roads are now excellent.

August 14, 1846

The foot regiment of Texan volunteers refuse to clear their camping ground. They are to be discharged Friday.[15] Harrison[16] arrived today. He is adjutant of the lst Regiment of Ohio Volunteers.

August 15, 1846

Was officer of the day.

August 15, 1846

The transportation for the army is to be one [burro] for every eight men and one for the officers of each company.

August 15, 1846

"Captain Lamotte and I went to church today to hear the Reverend Mr. Rey say mass ..."

Two wagons to a regiment for the hospital and ammunition. Our trunks are to be left. Captain Lamotte and I went to church today to hear the Reverend Mr. Rey[17] say mass and afterwards went on board of a steamboat to see if we send our trunks to the U. S. Took a Brigadier General of Volunteers to be Captain of the boat. [Dilworth note: The same general told Bliss that the country would stand to see the regulars in the.......(sentence not finished)]

In the evening I was standing near my tent when an individual came up and asked for me. I found him to be a Galveston lawyer and a Lieutenant of Volunteers. He had a letter from Mr. Buchanan, the Secretary of State. He was originally from Bedford, Pa. and knew E. The Post Office came up today.

August 17, 1846

Two General courts martial sit today: one in 7th Infantry stationed in town for the trial of First Lieutenant Hobson[18] of the 7th for drunkenness; the other in the 3rd Brigade for the trial of deserters.[19] Heard [had?] a review[20] of thirty-four companies. It was magnificent.

August 18, 1846

The Artillery Battalion crossed this day. There is to be a depot established at Cerralvo sixty miles from this by the way of Mier. The organization is as follows:

> First Division, Brigadier General Twiggs, Commanding 3rd Brigade (3rd & 4th Infantry), Lieutenant Colonel Garland 4th Brigade (1st & 2nd Infantry), Lieutenant Colonel Riley[21] Ridgeley's[22] Company of Light Artillery Regular Cavalry

Second Division, Brevet Brigadier General Worth, Commanding
lst Brigade (Artillery Battalion & 8th Infantry)
2nd Brigade (5th & 7th Infantry) Colonel Smith Commanding
Duncan's Artillery and Wood's Regiment of Texas Rangers[23]

Colonel Smith of the Regiment of Mounted Riflemen came up yesterday, and took command of the 2nd Brigade.

August 19, 1846

Was placed on special duty today to copy a map of the country from this to Saltillo.[24] Drew it in the village.

August 20, 1846

Finished the map.

August 22, 1846

In the evening of this day we marched into the village to relieve the 7th Infantry in the plaza, who, with the 5th, had crossed the river.

August 23, 1846

I marched on guard in the morning. It was the most disagreeable tour of duty that I ever performed. The day was excessively hot, and the atmosphere was full of dust. There were six inches of dust on the Plaza.[25] Early in the morning four regiments of volunteers and a train of 180 wagons passed through it, which raised a cloud that did not disappear during

August 19, 1846

"[I] was placed on special duty today to copy the map of the country from this [place] to Saltillo."

the whole day. There was a continued passing of horsemen and foot. Wagons, artillery carriages, and detachments of cavalry.

August 24, 1846

One of the duties of the Officer of the Guard was to see, when a steamboat arrived, that no persons who did not belong to the army came ashore without the written permission of General Taylor.[26] This morning at three o'clock a private steamboat came up loaded with sutlers and sutler's goods. There were also two or three other individuals, one having goods for sale and another a professed gambler. I placed a sentinel on the shore with orders for no one to come off the boat, but the sutlers. I went and reported the facts to the Lieutenant Colonel, as the Officer of the Day was sleeping. The day previous we had orders that Lieutenant Kane,[27] who had a detachment of Dragoon recruits, would relieve us this day. Reported the circumstances to the Lieutenant Colonel that there were persons on board the boat who had not General Taylor's permission to land and I wished for further orders on this. "Oh," he replied, "carry out the General's orders as they were written out for the command."

"I have sir," I replied, "and wish to know what else is to be done."

He thought for awhile and then said, "By G-d, I'll turn the command over to Lieutenant Kane."

"In the meantime," said I, "What orders shall I give the sentinel?"

"Just go up, Mr. D and report the circumstances to General Taylor." And by this means he managed [to] throw all responsibility from himself, wishing in the first place to throw it on a lieutenant.

We commenced crossing the San Juan on the steamboat Aid. We engaged a dinner on board, but after waiting a long while, found that we were not to have it. Got into camp at two P.M. I recrossed the river and called on General Hamer,[28] the Volunteer's general from Ohio. Returning at night, I passed through the camp of the 7th. They were to leave the next morning, and although it was nine P.M., they were in high glee and had not begun to pack their things for a march at three A.M. Captain Miller of the lst was there, and after remaining for some time, we both got on the same horse, but the Captain took a road leading from our camp. As soon as we were past the sentinels chain, we started at full speed down a road which led into a wagon trail. The teamsters who were sleeping near their wagons saw us coming and picking up their blankets ran in between the wheels of their wagons for protection calling out, "You can't get through here; you'll kill yourselves," but away we went at a fast pace, pushing the mules around and making a perfect commotion.

We got out of this train safe and charged another, and were going down the road at a gallop when our horse fell and threw us some distance over his head to the amusement of numerous teamsters and quarter-master's men. After a few more charges we got back safe to the camp.

August 28, 1846

No news of the 2nd Infantry except a report that they were off the Brazos [Santiago].

I walked up the bank of the river about a mile and came into a village called New Camargo.[29] I entered a house in which there were a man and woman. I noticed that they were unusually reserved, particularly as it appeared to be the house of an American, for in one corner was a surveyor's compass, and on the table a case of surveyor's instruments and several English books. There were also two or three very white and intelligent looking children in the house. I asked the boy his name and he said it was "Antonio Carabajal." He was the son of the notorious Carabajal.[30]

August 28, 1846

I visited an Indian village, which is about 200 yards back of our camp. They were greaser Indians, and finer looking men I never saw. They were encamped on a rocky hill. The rock was composed of sand and lime, principally sand. There was much crystallized gypsum amongst it.

August 29, 1846

An order has been issued today that the 3rd Brigade and lst Infantry would march on Monday, the thirty-first, for Mier. General Worth and the lst Brigade are at Cerralvo. Persons who returned with the train say that there are any number of clear, cool mountain streams off the road full of trout, but that the dust is full one foot deep on the road.

August 30, 1846

It rained, a sure sign that we are to march. A report has reached us of a resolution in favor of Santa Anna.[31]

August 31, 1846

Captain Lamotte came to my tent at midnight with a letter from ———— [line incomplete] Last night an orderly came over from General Twiggs with an order for us to move this morning. All ready for starting, but the muleteer we sent over to the village, and he is not back yet. The Lieutenant Colonel gave him permission to go if he could get a mule changed for him. The Colonel's mule would not pack, and he wanted one of the Quarter Master's.

We marched nine miles today. We had everything ready for packing on the mules when the order came for our movements to be delayed until further orders. The reason of the delay was the non-arrival of the 2nd Infantry, with whom we were brigaded. We were, however, temporarily to be brigaded with the battalion of Baltimore Volunteers[32] who had not yet crossed the river. Lieutenants King[33] and Plummer of the lst left for the U.S. today in the steamer Natchez.[34] Both were sick.

SEPTEMBER

September 1, 1846

The third brigade marched today, and the Baltimore Battalion crossed the river.

September 2, 1846

At eleven A.M. General Taylor and Twiggs came into camp, and we received orders to march immediately.

The mules began to be packed, but we were unable to get off before three P.M. We marched one and one-half miles and encamped on the bank of the river. The Hatchee Eagle[1] that went down yesterday returned this evening. Presuming that she brought important news, Lieutenant Terrett and myself got permission to return to the village. The Lieutent Colonel told us as soon as the Volunteers came up, he would go on, if he had to march all night, for General Twiggs had ordered him to get to

Camp Butler nine miles that night. After going a short distance we met the Volunteers coming down the road, two or three companies singing "Get Along, Josey."[2]

I wished to return, but I knew it was impossible for them to strike the tents in less than two hours, and in that time we could get back. We crossed the river and found King and Plummer. The boat had gone down the river nearly to Reynosa and had taken troops from a boat that had been two weeks on the way.

There was no mail. Returning, we lost our way and got some distance from the river, but getting on the top of a small hill, we could see in the moonlight. We could see our camp extending for two miles on the other bank of the river. We did not leave our camp until after sundown, but returning, there was a fine moon. Terrett wished to return to the ferry and make a new start, but I persuaded him to go towards the river, and we soon found the road and in a moment were in our camp.

They had not left, as I had predicted. The Volunteers were sleeping without blankets or tents. Their commander would not let them pitch tents, on account of the length of time it took them to get ready. Lieutenant Booker[3] and Snellen [Soulard][4] of the lst came down from Cerralvo with the return train. General Worth had sent them to Camargo to get their uniforms.

September 3, 1846

Reveille beat at two A.M., and we marched at four. The road was very dusty. About six o'clock came to the Rio Grande. At eight we arrived at Camp Butler, where there were three companies of Light Artillery and two [of] Dragoons. General Twiggs commanding. We remained till four P.M. There was a most beautiful arroyo of clear water, very cool (for this climate), and then marched about four or five miles and encamped at a Rancho[5] on the bank of the Rio Grande. The river at both places where it has been seen today is very rapid.

September 4, 1846

Reveille at four, marched at six. The road touched the river twice and crossed two or three arroyos of cool water. We encamped at eleven A.M., three miles from Mier,[6] twenty miles from Camargo. Had a view here of the Sierra Madre in the blue distance. The peaks here distinctly outlined on the sky, far away to the west. The country in that direction is perfectly level so that mountains appear to rise directly from the plain, into which they gradually sink towards the south. But in the north they are hidden by the hills of Mier. There was never anything which———[sentence incomplete]

The reason for our encamping so early today was that it was eight miles to the next water. The country is becoming quite uneven, and drift formation is beginning to make its appearance. In fact, from the stratification visible in some of the arroyos, all of the level low country seems to be of the drift formation. The hills are of solid rock of lime or sandstone.

Major Abercrombie and Captain Lamotte went into Mier and on their return reported it to be one of the handsomest places we have been. They heard that General Worth's command had made prisoner of Canales.

September 5, 1846

Marched at five A.M. At about three miles we found good water and plenty of it. Saw Mier about three miles off. Then took direction directly towards the mountain, which became more and more distinct. The country was quite uneven, and we crossed one or two arroyos which would be very difficult for wagons to pass. Marched eighteen and one-half miles and encamped on the bank of a rapid and deep stream. It evidently came from the mountains, for it was full of drift wood and was quite cool.

About three miles from Mier we saw some red sandstone on the top of a hill. The rocks begin to dip from the mountain, and the appearance of the primary stratified. We saw some stone a short time before we came to the red sandstone and the gray sandstone shortly after. Met several boulders, which continued to get larger towards evening.

We encamped at half past eleven A.M. and took a fine bath. On the bank of the stream on which our camp was placed there were several large ash trees, the first forest trees that we have met with that grow in the North.

September 6, 1846

Spent a horrible night for the volunteers were awake and making their usual noise all night. We had a very severe march of at least fifteen miles and got into camp at Puntiagudo[7] at eleven A.M. There was one of the finest bathing places here that I have seen in this country. A fine stone dam, with stone side walls for irrigating the country, had a constant fall of water over it, a clear cool stream. [Dilworth's note: An express came from General Worth on the evening of the sixth saying he expected an attack on Cerralvo. Our muskets were loaded, and we were held in readiness to march.]

September 7, 1846

Went into the town. It was a place very much like Burrita, but much larger.

The reports from above are that the Mexicans are determined to fight at Monterey. There was no alarm last night, although we were turned out after tattoo to load our muskets. This camp is commanded by Lieutenant Colonel Garland, who is in command also of the 3rd Brigade, which is here. The 2nd left the morning that we arrived. Went to a fandango[8] and danced on the Plaza until two o'clock A.M. It was a fine moonlight night, and there were fifty females on the ground.

September 8, 1846

General Taylor and Twiggs with Ridgeley, Bragg's, Webster's,[9] and Mackall's[10] batteries of light artillery, and the 2nd Dragoons came in today. The whole of the lst Division is now here, and leave tomorrow morning at daylight. Went to another fandango.

September 9, 1846

Was very sick, and had to ride in a bagg[age] wagon. Yesterday an order containing promotions was brought into camp. I am promoted to the First Lieutenant. Capt. May[11] is made a Brevet Lieutenant Colonel for services on both the eighth and ninth of May, although he did nothing on the eighth. Duncan is made the same for the same reason, and did nothing on the ninth. Ridgely is made a Brevet Captain and distinguished himself on both days. Our route today was very slow, being uphill and having to cross one or two streams. The rear was very much detained, till the whole of the right wing had watered.

September 10, 1846

We arrived at Cerralvo[12] in the afternoon between one and two. It is the handsomest town that we have seen yet. The water is cool and clear. A number of springs near our camp send streams through nearly all the streets of the place. There is also a very fine-looking church. Near camp are some very large cypress trees. Still hear reports of Monterey being very strongly fortified.

General Hamer came in today with his Brigade. I received my commission of First Lieutenant. Heard that Harney[13] was arrested by General Wool[14] for leaving San Antonio without orders, as we had heard at New Orleans, leaving some thirty of his men at Presidio Rio Grande as a guard for stores. The inhabitants had risen on them and massacred all except one, who escaped to tell the tale.

September 11, 1846

The order of march came out today. The substance of it was that as we could not expect to go much farther without meeting resistance. The marches hereafter would be conducted with the greatest caution. The First Division would march on the thirteenth, and the Second and Field Divisions of Volunteers on successive days. All of the Pioneers of the army go tomorrow, guarded by a squadron of Dragoons.

September 12, 1846

The Pioneers left today.

September 13, 1846

We marched this morning, our line being directed towards the mountains. Had to wade several streams. The country here is very broken and rocky. We encamped twelve miles from Cerralvo.

September 14, 1846

My company was on the rear guard. It was very late before we could get the mules up. We started at ten. Marched about two miles and had to remain till twelve waiting for the packs to come up. Before we left camp, Colonel Smith[15] of Regiment of Riflemen came up with the advance of the Second Division.

Our road was very bad, and it was near dark before we got into camp. The mountains during the day were on our right, but we were entering a pass between them. When we got into camp, we heard of Captain McCullough's company of Rangers, who were in advance of the Pioneers, meeting 200 Mexican Lancers at Ramos[16] eight miles from us. They exchanged shots. The Rangers had one horse wounded. The enemy also [had] one horse and two men [wounded]. The Rangers were but fifty, but the Mexicans, wisely thinking that they were but the advance of the army, withdrew.

Our encampment was in the chapparal on a small stream of very bad water. We expect to meet the enemy at Marin[17] about seventeen miles from this. These are said to be fortified at a pass near there.

September 15, 1846

Our march today was through a most delightful country. Our road was in a valley between two mountains and presented some of the finest landscapes imaginable. We crossed several clear streams. One of them was almost a river. Occasionally we could see the head of our column far off in the distance, so far that we could not distinguish horse from foot. Our progress was slow and tedious, having several times to halt to clear the road from the artillery. When we arrived at Ramos, we found that nearly all the inhabitants had been driven off by the Lancers. The few [who] were left say that "there were many Mexican soldiers there yesterday, who were now at Marin."[18] Marin was but six miles off, and we pushed rapidly ahead. It was the middle of the afternoon when the cupola of the church was visible. When we saw the advanced guard must have been there, but as it was all quiet, we began to think that this was another bloodless victory. As we approached the town, all was as still as death, but there was no firing. The town was perfectly deserted. There were not ten families in the place. The Mexican troops to the amount of about 2000 had left about three hours before we entered. The Rangers came up in advance, and the Lancers formed line in the square to wait for them; but after waiting for some time they left. Torrejon[19] commanded. In the morning a Mexican had been found with a pass of General [Zachary] Taylor's in his possession and was taken out and shot. We passed through the town and encamped two miles from it. Was on guard during the night.

September 16, 1846

The Second Division came up today. Our encampment is on the San Juan. Reports say that they are still fortifying Monterey. We are entirely surrounded by mountains. The prospect at—— [incomplete sentence]

September 17, 1846

Went into the town and had a view of Monterey. Two Mexican deserters came in today and report that they are going to fight us. Ampudia is in command. We march tomorrow, the advanced guard [leaving] at half past five A.M. The first division at six; 2nd at seven, and Division of Volunteers at eight A.M. The order of battle is to be as follows: lst Div. on the right; 2nd on the left; and Vol in the center. The volunteers came in today.

September 18, 1846

We marched according to the order. Our route lay directly towards the mountains. It has [been] very dusty and no air stirring. At about thirteen miles from Marin we came to a very handsome country seat called Agua Fria[20] and encamped at a village of the same name about two miles nearer Monterey.

As our advanced guard entered the place, the streets were full of Lancers under Torrejon, who fled when our Dragoons gave chase. They, however, escaped. We found several proclamations from General Ampudia to the U. S. Army [advising] them to lay down their arms and they would be well treated. Our camp was supplied with water by several small artificial streams running through it, but after a short time the water was found to have ceased to flow; the cause was that the Mexicans turned off the water above.

Went into the village. The whole army had come in, and the volunteers were stripping and pillaging everything. Four were caught endeavoring to break into a house, and General Taylor ordered them to be [arrested] and sent home.[21] A Mexican was also taken up supposed to be a spy and taken to General Worth but three times attempted to escape. The second time he was

September 19, 1846

"I was in a tree top and could see the flag in the city."

wounded in the head with a knife, but the third he got some distance and a crowd got around him and beat his brains out.

September 19, 1846

We commenced our march at sunrise this morning and at twenty-five minutes past nine A.M. heard a twelve pounder fire at Monterey. Two other discharges were made in quick succession and in a short time two more. At the sound our men stepped off almost in a run. We were about three miles from the city. In about two miles we came to a halt and found the advance returning to encamp in the rear for there was no water to be found in front except under the guns of the city. (We found today all the streams that crossed the road had been turned off and the bridges destroyed.) As the Dragoons passed us, Sacket[22] asked me if I heard the "Elephant" groan[23] in Monterey. We were then told that the Texas Rangers who had joined us yesterday were in advance and had passed up and had a skirmish with some Lancers and General Taylor was a short distance in the rear of the Rangers. After seeing that there was no water, he turned with his staff to return when a battery opened on them. A twelve pound ball struck the ground a short distance from them and bouncing came about ten feet from the General. I saw the ball. It was iron. They have got out of copper. Some twelve shots were fired at the Rangers when they ceased. We encamped[24] in a woods of pecan trees about three miles from the city.

At four o'clock P.M. Capt. Williams's[25] Top Eng went out with a Company of Dragoons and Texas Rangers to reconnoiter. I was in a tree top and could see the flag in the city. At one-half past four I saw the smoke curl up from a gun, and in short time the report came to me. They were firing at Captain Williams' party. Returning to camp, I met Generals Taylor, Twiggs, and Worth going out to reconnoiter.

September 19, 1846

"As the Dragoons passed us, Sackett asked me if I heard the 'Elephant' groan in Monterrey."

CONCLUSION

Dilworth's narrative ends abruptly with his entry on September 19, the day Taylor's army reached Monterrey. Dilworth was mortally wounded on September 21, 1846, "by a twelve-pounder cannon ball"[1] that tore off one leg. He was engaged in the diversionary attack on the eastern side of Monterrey with his regiment and must have been caught in the crossfire. Dilworth lived only long enough to hear of the great American victory, dying on September 27, 1846, at the age of twenty-four.

The bodies of many of the wealthier or more famous American soldiers were returned from Mexico to the United States for formal burials in their hometowns. But alas, Rankin Dilworth was neither wealthy nor famous, and his body was most probably consigned to a soldier's grave. The Office of the Adjutant General received a letter from Dilworth's mother[2] requesting his personal effects that must have undoubtedly included this journal, but there is no formal indication that his body was returned to the United States.

William S. Henry, an army officer, on a visit to the eastern side of Monterrey in October 1846, recorded these thoughts:[3]

> In going over the eastern extremity of the city, and seeing the number of barricades, fortified houses, and redoubts, it is inconceivable how so many escaped the first day's [September 21] fight. It was here the fierce battle raged, and all around are the graves of the noble dead. Strange how some of the brightest flowers of the army should have been selected! Morris, Barbour, Field, Irwin, Hoskins, Woods, Hazlitt, Terrett, Dilworth, Williams! Brave and gallant spirits! Each of you have a soldier's sepulcher, and a page in the history of your country's glory.

The bodies of these fallen soldiers were removed from their shallow graves on the east side of Monterrey on November 25, 1846, and reburied in a solemn ceremony conducted by the troops.[4] The bodies were interred in a dignified cemetery constructed by the Third Infantry. The cemetery[5] "is a square inclosure, situated a few yards to the west of the road leading to Monterey, and directly in front of the camp of the regiment. The wall is four feet high, and on the face toward the camp there is a rectangular pillar surmounted by a cross. It is built of blocks of white limestone neatly dressed."

In 1965, private parties[6] conducted a survey of the Monterrey battle sites. They concluded that the cemetery was probably located in the vicinity of Ojo Nogal, just west of the old road to Marin. There remains one small cemetery near Ojo Nogal, which satisfies Henry's description, but it has only

Mexican headstones. However, it is a common practice in Mexico to rebury over existing gravesites, and this could be the case. The growth of the city and the amount of new construction in this vicinity of Monterrey has probably covered over this little site containing the graves of foreign invaders.

Classmates of Dilworth at West Point who also became casualties of the Mexican War were: Erastus Burton Strong and William Trumbull Burwell at Molino del Rey, September 8, 1847; James Sterrett Woods at Monterrey, September 21, 1846; Joseph Poinsett Smith at Chapultepec, on September 13, 1847. Mortally wounded at Molino del Rey was George Wainwright, who died in New York on August 2, 1848.

Two other classmates died in the Civil War: Frances John Thomas at Bull Run on July 21, 1861, at age 37, and Alexander Hayes in the Wilderness, on May 5, 1864.

The War with Mexico served a purpose, albeit a frightful one. Here was the training ground for many of the officers who would serve, and die, on both sides of the fighting during the Civil War.

How bizarre it must have been for these officers, veterans of fighting together, to face each other on American battlefields. War makes strange enemies, and comrades.

NOTES

INTRODUCTION

1. The United States Military Academy was one of the finest universities in the United States in the early and mid-nineteenth century, and trained the vast majority of professional engineers found in the country. The surprisingly balanced curriculum offered a cadet was, in part, as follows:

   Fourth Class
   Mathematics Algebra, Geometry, Descriptive Geometry
   French
   Third Class
   Mathematics Projections and warped surfaces, Surveying,
   Analytical Geometry, Calculus
   French
   Drawing Human Figure, Topography
   Ethics
   Second Class
   Natural Science Mechanics, Electricity and Magnetism,
   Electro-magnetism, Electro-dynamics,
   Optics, Astronomy
   Chemistry

Drawing Landscape, Topography
First Class
Engineering and
Science of War Field Fortifications, Permanent
Fortifications, Attack and Defense, Mines,
Composition of Armies, Strategy, Civil
Engineering, Architecture, Stone Cutting,
Machines
Ethics Rhetoric, Moral Philosophy, Constitution of the United States
Infantry Tactics
Artillery
Mineralogy and Geology
Official Register of the Officers and Cadets of the U. S. Military Academy, West Point, New-York, June 1841-1844.

APRIL

1. Robert Selden Garnett graduated from the United States Military Academy in 1841 and was assigned to the 4th Artillery throughout the Mexican War. He was cited for "gallant conduct in the several conflicts at Monterrey, Mexico" and for "gallantry and meritorious conduct in the battle of Buena Vista, Mexico." Garnett resigned from the service on April 30, 1861, and died July 13, 1861, in action at Carricks Ford, Virginia, at the rank of brigadier general, CSA. Francis B. Heitman, *Historical Register and Dictionary of the United States Army, From Its Organization, September 29, 1789, to March 2, 1903* (Washington: Government Printing Office, 1903), 1: 447. (Cited hereafter as Heitman, *Register.*)

2. Benjamin Walker was a graduate of the United States Military Academy in 1819, rising to the rank of major in 1839, as a paymaster. He died on May 28, 1858. Heitman, *Register,* 2: 995.

3. John Chapman Terrett was a Virginian who enlisted in the 1st Infantry at the rank of second lieutenant on November 16, 1839. He was killed in action on September 21, 1846, during the capture of Monterrey, Mexico. Heitman, *Register,* 1: 951.

4. The eve of actual hostilities found the United States Army with its smallest effective force since 1808, about 5,300 men. This cadre was distributed among eight regiments of infantry, two of dragoons, and four of artillery. In 1842, Congress, in a spirit of retrenchment, re-

duced the permissable size of an infantry company to forty-two men. Thus the undermanned 1st Infantry had to consolidate its small companies into an effective fighting force. Companies F and I were broken up and the men used to beef up the ranks of companies C, E, and K. After war against Mexico had been declared, on May 13, 1846, Congress reset company troop strength at 100 men. The active recruiting efforts for volunteer regiments occuring then created a competition for men that prevented most army companies from ever being manned at full strength. William A. Ganoe, *The History of the United States Army* (Ashton, Md: Eric Lundberg, 1964) 196-200; R. S. Ripley, *The War with Mexico*, (New York: Burt Franklin, 1970), 2: 94-96.

5. Henry Wilson was a Pennsylvanian who enlisted in the army in May 1813 at the rank of ensign. He served at the rank of lieutenant-colonel in the 1st Infantry throughout the Mexican War. Wilson was cited for "gallantry and meritorious conduct in the several conflicts at Monterey, Mexico." He resigned from the service on February 25, 1861. Heitman, *Register*, 1: 1046.

6. John Joseph Abercrombie graduated from the United States Military Academy in 1822. During the Mexican War, he served as a captain in the 1st Infantry until September 8,1847, when he was transferred to the 5th Infantry at the rank of major. He was cited for gallantry and meritorious conduct for his actions at the capture of Monterrey. Abercrombie served as brigadier general of volunteers in the Union Army from 1861 to 1865, retiring from the service in 1865. Heitman, *Register*, 1: 150.

7. John Henry Miller graduated from the United States Military Academy in 1833 and was assigned to the 4th Artillery. He was cited for meritorious conduct in the defense of Pueblo, Mexico, on October 12, 1847, and died at the rank of captain on September 12, 1850. Heitman, *Register*, 1: 711.

8. Electus Backus graduated from the United States Military Academy in 1824 and was assigned to the 1st Infantry. He served throughout the Mexican War in this regiment and was cited for gallant conduct at the capture of Monterrey. Backus died on June 7, 1862, at the rank of colonel. Heitman, *Register*, 1: 179.

9. Joseph Hatch La Motte graduated from the United States Military Academy in 1827 and served throughout the Mexican War in the 1st Infantry at the rank of captain. He was cited for gallant conduct at the capture of Monterrey for his actions on September 23, 1846. La Motte

resigned from the service on October 31, 1856. Heitman, *Register,* 1: 613.

10. Thomas John Wood graduated from the United States Military Academy in 1845 and was assigned to the topographical engineers. He transferred to the 2d Dragoons, in October 1846, and remained in that unit throughout the Mexican War. He was cited for gallantry at the battle of Buena Vista on February 23, 1847. Wood rose to the rank of major general in the Union Army and was cited for gallantry and meritorious conduct at the battles of Chickamauga and Nashville. He retired from the service in 1875. Heitman, *Register,* 1: 1055.

11. William Farquhar Barry graduated from the United States Military Academy in 1838 and was assigned to the 4th Artillery. He was transferred to the 2d Artillery in which he served throughout the Mexican War. He rose to the rank of brigadier general of volunteers in the Union Army and was cited for his actions at the capture of Atlanta and the Atlanta Campaign for "gallant and meritorious service in the field during the war" and "for gallant and meritorious service in the campaign terminating with the surrender of the insurgent army under Gen. J. E. Johnston." Barry died on July 17, 1879. Heitman, *Register,* 1: 195.

12. Stephen Decatur Carpenter graduated from the United States Military Academy in 1840 and served in the 1st Infantry throughout the Mexican War. He rose to the rank of colonel in the Union Army, being cited for his actions at the battles of Shiloh and Murfreesboro. Carpenter was killed in action at Murfreesboro on December 31, 1862. Heitman, *Register,* 1: 284.

13. Samuel Moses Plummer graduated from the United States Military Academy in 1835 and served in the 1st Infantry throughout the Mexican War at the rank of captain. He died on October 17, 1851. Heitman, *Register,* 1: 795.

14. William R. Jouett was commissioned as a second lieutenant in the 1st Infantry on February 19, 1818. He had risen to the rank of captain by May 1, 1829, and was serving at the rank of lieutenant-colonel in the 3rd Infantry when he died on May 1, 1852. Heitman, *Register,* 1: 584.

15. Ferdinand Suydan Mumford graduated from the United States Military Academy in 1838 and served in the 1st Infantry throughout the Mexican War. He resigned from the service on August 31, 1849. Heitman, *Register,* 1: 735.

16. Frederick H. Masten joined the service in 1838 and was assigned to the 1st Infantry at the rank of lieutenant. He resigned from the service on December 31, 1857. Heitman, *Register,* 1: 696.

17. Col. William Davenport, commander of the 1st Infantry, had joined the service in 1812, and his advanced age probably made him unable to assume a field command. The military service at that time had no provision for retirement, and officers that should have been superannuated continued on some form of duty until death. The colonel and the regimental band were probably detached for a recruiting mission to bolster the thin ranks of the 1st Infantry, which had been decimated by peacetime politics. Davenport resigned from the service on January 31, 1850 and died on April 12, 1858. Heitman, *Register,* 1: 355.

18. Leonidas Jenkins graduated from the United States Military Academy in 1841 and was assigned to duty in the 1st Dragoons. He died on October 18, 1847. Heitman, *Register,* 1: 572.

19. On July 10, 1826, Maj. Stephen W. Kearny, with four companies of the 1st Infantry, established a camp below St. Louis on the Mississippi River. The camp was named "Cantonment Adams" in honor of the current president, but the adjutant general ordered it to be renamed "Jefferson Barracks" in honor of the third president, who had recently died. This site was to become an "Infantry School of Practice" where newly commissioned lieutenants would receive basic training. This site was evidently moved by General Gaines in 1827 to a site near the mouth of the Missouri River, not far from the village of Vide Porche. Gaines did not wish to place the barracks in nearby St. Louis because an environment would be created "around which the dregs of a mixed population, with whiskey shops and other nuisances might be brought into close contact with the soldiery." This post served as an important link between the East and the frontier for many decades. Haskell M. Monroe, Jr. and James T. McIntosh, *The Papers of Jefferson Davis* (Baton Rouge: LSU Press, 1971) 1: 106; and James W. Silver, *Edmund Pendleton Gaines, Frontier General* (Baton Rouge: LSU Press, 1949), 99.

MAY

1. John F. Jones was Rankin Dilworth's brother-in-law, husband of his sister Abigail.

2. The play was likely one performed by Charles and Ellen Tree Kean, theatrical personalities widely known in the United States and England for acting and producing plays, especially those of Shakespeare, which he altered and revised, apparently to the dislike of some. Between 1845 and 1847, he made his third American tour. See Oscar G. Brockett, *History of the Theatre* (Boston: Allyn and Bacon, 1968), 430-32.

3. Prairie Du Chien is located on the Mississippi River near the confluence with the Wisconsin River about ninety miles west of present-day Madison, Wisconsin. It was the scene of fighting between settlers and various Indian groups, including Winnebagos, Patawatomis, Ottawas, Sioux, and others. Apparently Dilworth had once been stationed there.

4. This person was most likely William H. Hurst, editor of the Vicksburg newspaper, *Southern Intelligencer,* which later merged, about the time of the Mexican War, with the *Sentinel and Expositor,* also of Vicksburg. As editor, in those pre-telegraph days, it was his duty to meet arriving steamboats and question the travelers for news items that might be of use in his paper. In exchange, he evidently supplied the latest news of the Mexican War to Dilworth. James T. McIntosh, *The Papers of Jefferson Davis* (Baton Rouge: LSU Press, 1974), 2: 376.

5. Capt. Seth Thornton's squadron of the 2d Dragoons was ambushed by Mexican forces of Gen. Anastasio Torrejón on the morning of April 26, 1846, at Rancho de Carricitos. Eleven American troopers were killed and six wounded. The remainder, including Capt. Thornton, were captured by the Mexicans. After several prior clashes with the Mexicans, this incident forced Taylor to conclude that "hostilities may now be considered as commenced" and was referred to in Polk's declaration of War address to Congress: "American blood has been spilled on American soil." Thornton and the other Mexican prisoners were returned after the battles of May 8 and 9. Thornton was ordered before a court-martial for his actions in this skirmish and was honorably acquitted of all charges. He was killed August 18, 1847, while on a reconnaissance near the San Antonio Valley of Central Mexico. Heitman, *Register,* 1: 959; Bauer, *The Mexican War,* 1846-1848, 48.

6. Lt. Elias Kent Kane of the 2d Dragoons survived and in fact was captured by the Mexicans, but Lt. George Thompson Mason of the 2d Dragoons was killed in the skirmish at Rancho de Carricitos on April 26, 1846. Heitman, *Register,* 1: 585, 695.

7. Capt. William Hardee, second in command of Thornton's squadron, surrendered himself and the remaining men to the Mexicans after promise of honorable treatment. Dana reports a letter from Hardee, then a prisoner, stating that "they [Hardee and Kane] were living at the table of General Ampudia in Matamoros and treated with as much kindness and politeness as they could desire. They were allowed to send for their baggage and servants, and when they wanted to make some arrangements about their pay, they were told by General Arista that they need not trouble themselves about that, that whilst they were prisoners the Mexican government would advance them half their monthly pay and only on the honor of our government to refund." Hardee and Kane were exchanged by the Mexican Army prior to its evacuation of Matamoros. Hardee requested and received a court of inquiry concerning his actions in the surrender and was found to have acted honorably. Robert H. Ferrell, *Monterrey Is Ours! The Mexican War Letters of Lieutenant Dana, 1845-1847* (Lexington: University Press of Kentucky, 1990), 56.

8. The man referred to by Dilworth is probably Lt. George Thompson Mason, killed by the Mexicans during the ambush.

9. In a letter of May 20, 1846, to the adjutant general of the army, Taylor acknowledged that "On the 26th of April [1846],...I found it necessary to use the authority with which I was vested, and call upon the governors of Louisiana and Texas for a force each of four regiments....It is extremely doubtful whether the foot regiments from Texas can be raised, and I shall desire the governor, who is expected here [Matamoros], to suspend the call for them." Ex. Doc. 60, [No. 42]

10. Gen. Edmund P. Gaines was in charge of the Western Military District of the United States, with headquarters in New Orleans. In August 1845, rumors of the encirclement of Taylor's forces at Corpus Christi by a strong Mexican force prompted Gaines to take unauthorized actions. He contacted the governors of Louisiana and Alabama to requisition volunteers he felt were needed for Taylor's defense. There was no legal authority for his actions, and even when ordered by the adjutant general of the army to cease and desist, Gaines continued to request volunteer regiments from state officials. Before his recruiting efforts could be halted, more than 6,000 volunteers from the state of Louisiana alone were mustered by him into federal service for a period of six months. By the Militia Act of 1795, volunteers were obliged to serve only a three-month term. This unexpected flood of volunteers created massive supply problems for Taylor, requiring tents and

hardtack then in scarce supply in south Texas. With the massive cost to the taxpayer created by their enlistment, they barely reached the shores of south Texas before their enlistment expired, and had to be shipped on a return trip to New Orleans. Gaines was called before a court-martial on 14 August 1846, to answer charges of misuse of his authority. Gaines was found guilty, but the tribunal recommended that "in view of his long services and his undoubted patriotism and purity of motives, no disciplinary action be taken." President Polk upheld the findings of the court. James W. Silver, *Edmund Pendleton Gaines, Frontier General* (Baton Rouge: LSU Press, 1949) 258-67.

11. Construction on the magnificent St. Charles Hotel was begun in 1836. Under the supervision of the Irish architect Gallier, a structure rose on the site two squares away from Canal Street of which the city could be justly proud. The facade had a projecting portico of fourteen Corinthian columns topped by a tall marble pediment. A circular colonnade of heavy marble supported a white dome topped by an open turret. For the more practical traveler there was a magnificent oval barroom seventy feet across and twenty feet high that was reached by a double flight of stairs. A traveler reported that the St. Charles was "not only the largest and handsomest hotel in the United States, but the largest and handsomest hotel in the world." This marvelous building burned in 1851; the present St. Charles Hotel occupies the site. Harnett T. Kane, *Queen New Orleans: City by the River* (New York: Bonanza Books, 1949), 136-40.

12. On a steamship a hurricane deck is either a light upper deck or a bridge located amidships.

13. The *Hannibal* was a sidewheel packet steamer with a wooden hull. She was built in Elizabeth, Pennsylvania in 1844 and listed Port St. Louis as her first home port. Fred Way, Jr., *Way's Packet Directory: 1848-1983* (Athens: Ohio University Press, 1983), 337.

14. The *Galveston* was a sidewheel steamer of 548 tons, built in 1845 at New York. She was stranded and abandoned on November 25, 1851, at Ship Island, Mississippi. William R. Lytle and Forrest R. Holdcamper, *Merchant Steam Vessels of the United States: 1807-1868* (Staten Island, N.Y.: Steamship Historical Society of America, 1975), 78.

15. Philip Roots Thompson graduated from the United States Military Academy in 1835 and was assigned to the 1st Dragoons. He rose to the rank of captain during the Mexican War and was cited for his actions

in the battle of Sacramento, near Chihuahua. Thompson was cashiered from the service on September 4, 1855. Heitman, *Register,* 1: 957.

16. Mrs. Susan Dana was the wife of Lt. Napoleon Jackson Tecumseh Dana of the 7th Infantry. She had followed him from Jefferson Barracks in St. Louis to the barracks at New Orleans as he departed from there on April 1, 1846, for duty in Texas. She remained with friends at New Orleans Barracks for quite a while. For a lively and sometimes earthy account of love through the mails and an exciting account of the campaign in northern Mexico, see Ferrell, *Monterrey Is Ours.*

17. Stephen Decatur Dobbins was a cadet at the United States Military Academy in 1830 and again in 1834. In 1838, he was assigned to the 3d Infantry; he was dismissed from the service on December 1, 1847. Heitman, *Register,* 1: 375.

18. A sally port is a postern gate or an underground passage in a fortification that leads from the inner to the outer works which allows defenders egress for counterattacks.

19. The attack on Capt. Samuel H. Walker's camp by Mexican rancheros on the night of April 25, 1846, resulted in the deaths of five Texans. Of the eight posted to guard the camp, only three escaped: George Washington "Wash" Trahern, Maurice Simons, and the colorful Texan G. K. "Legs" Lewis. Simons related that the incident was brought on by the irascible Creed Taylor: "Taylor killed an old Mexican" much against the wishes of Simons, and in revenge that night, "we were attacked in camp by 200 Mexicans." Simons' widow, writing in later years to her daughter, said of the episode: "Once they [Maurice and Wash] and six men who went with them to drive the beeves were camped out when they heard Mexican soldiers. They ran undressed and barefooted, scattered in every direction. Maurice hid under some cactus and saw one of his men killed. A Mexican officer cut him open with a sword. The prickly pear was so dense that while he was there two of the Mexican soldiers stopped near enough to him to light their cigars and he could hear what they said. They were saying that they would rather have those two blackheaded devils (he and Wash) than all the others. He staid there until dark then made his way to headquarters where he found Wash who had made just as close an escape. J. E. Connor, "The Maurice Kavanaugh Simons Diary," unpublished MS, Texas A & I University Library.

20. The Balize, a lighthouse that marked the Southeast Pass of the Mississippi River, was surrounded by a "little cluster of laboriously anchored shacks" which housed the river pilots. Its location at the mouth of the river was characterized by travelers as exhibiting "the full sublimity of desolation." By the late nineteenth century, the main-traveled Southeast Pass became silted over, and shipping shifted to the Southwest Pass. Edwin Adams Davis, *The Rivers and Bayous of Louisiana* (Baton Rouge: Louisiana Education Research Assn., 1968), 147-49.

21. The *New York* was a wooden-hulled sternwheeler of 365 tons, built in New York in 1837. The ship, under the command of Captain Phillips, foundered and was lost on September 5, 1846, about seventy miles from Galveston on a run from that city to New Orleans. Seventeen lives were lost; survivors were rescued by the steamship *Galveston.* Lytle and Holdcamper, *Merchant Steam Vessels,*157; *American Flag,* 16-19 September 1846.

22. The Mexican cannonading of Fort Brown could be heard at Point Isabel, more than twenty miles away. Ulysses S. Grant, who was at Point Isabel, at that time remembered that "As we lay in our tents upon the sea-shore, the artillery at the fort on the Rio Grande could be distinctly heard....What General Taylor's feelings were during this suspense I do not know; but for myself, a young second-lieutenant who had never heard a hostile gun before, I felt sorry that I had enlisted." E. B. Long, *Personal Memoirs of U. S. Grant* (Cleveland: World Publishing Co., 1952) 42-43.

23. The *Alabama* was a sidewheel steamer of 676 tons owned by the United States Government and used during the Mexican War principally in the Gulf of Mexico to transport soldiers and supplies. The ship was lost on July 12, 1852, off Gun Key in the Bahamas. Erna Risch, *Quarter Master Support of the Army: A History of the Corps: 1775-1939* (Washington: Office of the Quarter Master General, 1962), 260.

24. Militiamen from the State of Louisiana were the first volunteers to arrive in south Texas in brigade strength. They came in response to a letter sent from Gen. Zachary Taylor to the governor of Louisiana in late April 1846 requesting additional troop strength. By the time the Louisiana contingent arrived in south Texas, the crisis had been resolved.

25. *Mania a potu* is a mental derangement resulting from the excessive use of intoxicants.

26. Point Isabel was a small village on the Laguna Madre, about five miles northwest of the Brazos Santiago Pass. This village, originally named Frontón, was a Mexican customs station serving as a port of entry for the city of Matamoros and a large portion of northeastern Mexico. An extensive supply depot was established there during the Mexican War, and an earthen defense, Fort Polk, was thrown up around the depot. The City of Port Isabel exists today on this site. The only remaining wall of Fort Polk forms an embankment upon which the lighthouse was built.

27. The *Augusta* was a sidewheel steamer of 290 tons, built in Cincinnati, Ohio, in 1835. Her first home port was Natchez, Mississippi. She was lost June 4, 1846, on the Brazos River of Texas in an accident that cost the lives of eight passengers and crew. Lytle and Holdcamper, *Steam Vessels*, 15.

28. The Brazos Island was a barrier island off the coast of south Texas bounded on the east and the west respectively by the Gulf of Mexico and the Laguna Madre, and on the north and south respectively by Brazos (de) Santiago (literally "the arms of Saint James") and Boca Chica (literally "little mouth," an ancient smaller mouth of the Rio Grande). The island extended for about three miles north of the mouth of the Rio Grande.

29. Padre Island is an immense barrier island on the Gulf of Mexico that extends from just south of Corpus Christi to the mouth of the Rio Grande.

30. St. Joseph's Island is the barrier island east of Corpus Christi.

31. John T. Price's company of Texas Mounted Volunteers was composed of personnel recruited in the Victoria and Goliad Counties of Texas. The company was sworn into federal service on September 25, 1845, reorganized on March 25, 1846, and mustered out of service on June 15, 1846. Price's Company marched from Corpus Christi to Point Isabel along the beach to avoid the chaparral country between the Nueces River and Rio Grande. This probably explains why they were sighted by Dilworth from the transport ship. Charles D. Spurlin, *Texas Veterans in the Mexican War* (Nacogdoches: Erickson Press, 1984), 200.

32. The Home Fleet of the United States Navy, under the command of Commodore Conner, patrolled the Gulf of Mexico. Their mission was to blockade the Mexican coast and assist the forces of Gen. Zachary Taylor. The fleet consisted of eleven frigates and sloops directed from the flagship *Cumberland*, of later Civil War fame. On May 6, 1846,

Conner landed some 1,200 "bluejackets" and marines to aid in the defense of Point Isabel. These men however were blissfully ignorant of company evolutions and the small arms drill. One of the naval officers would give the order "double up" when he wished to form two ranks. The young army officers fresh from West Point had many laughs at the expense of the navy. Young Abner Doubleday claimed that such commands as "Forward on the weatherbeam" and "Ship your bayonets" were voiced to the tars by their officers. The seamen declaimed to the many landsmen at Point Isabel that if the Mexicans came that "they ought to be allowed to board them." From Point Isabel, on May 8, the sound of booming guns carried from across the prairie as the Battle of Palo Alto progressed. A rumor spread among the sailors that Taylor had been defeated and the navy became eager to march to the rescue of the army. Commodore Conner refused the request from his officers on land to advance because he knew that if the unschooled navy forces were caught on the open prairie by Mexican cavalry they would be cut to pieces and his fleet would be undermanned. Capt. William Harwar Parker, *Recollections of a Naval Officer: 1841-1865* (New York: Charles Scribners' Sons, 1885), 50-51; and Abner Doubleday, "From the Mexican War to the Rebellion", MS, New-York Historical Society, New York, N.Y.

33. Barita, or Burrita, is a small Mexican village situated on a high bluff of the Rio Grande about ten miles from the mouth. A map of Mexican War vintage indicates only about eight huts in the village and a small American army camp.

34. The term *ranchero* was originally applied to the many cow hands and drovers that populated northern Mexico, but came to refer during the Mexican War to a group of lightly armed Mexican irregular cavalry that fought the guerrilla war waged in northern Mexico from 1846 to 1848. Their most novel weapon was the "lazo," a braided rawhide or horsehair lariat with a loop on the end used to snare cattle and unwary Americans. Most Americans had never seen a loop tossed from horseback to snare prey, either bovine or human, and marvelled at the dexterity of Mexican horsemen. These roping skills would later be adopted by the American cowboy who learned many of his ranching skills from his Mexican counterpart.

35. Interservice rivalries are not a recent phenomenonon of military life. Capt. William Parker, on duty with the Home Fleet off Brazos Santiago, was critical of the actions of his commander, Commodore

David Conner for not taking a more aggressive role in the battle of Palo Alto and other land actions during this time. He wrote

> In an interview between General Taylor and Commodore Conner it was agreed that there should be a combined attack upon a place called Burrita, on the Rio Grande. Colonel Wilson, with the First Infantry, was to march by land and we were to send a boat expedition up the river. We accordingly weighed and anchored off the mouth of the Rio Grande; but there being a rather heavy swell on the bar the commodore would not risk the boats. We waited two days, and on the third the expedition started under Captain Aulick. When he got to Burrita he found the First Infantry in quiet possession of it—so here was another disappointment to the navy and another opportunity lost.

Capt. William Harwar Parker, *Recollections of a Naval Officer: 1841-1865* (New York: Charles Scribners' Sons, 1885), 56.

36. Col. James B. Walton led the 1st Louisiana Volunteer Infantry. This regiment was illegaly mustered into service by Gen. Edmund P. Gaines and served in south Texas less than three months. Heitman, *Register,* 2: 71.

37. Charles Thomas enlisted as a third lieutenant of ordnance in 1819. Thomas served as a major in the quartermaster department during the Mexican War. He was cited on May 30, 1848, for "meritorious conduct while serving in the enemy's country." He rose to the rank of colonel in the Union Army and was cited for "faithful and meritorious service during the war" on March 13, 1865. Thomas retired from the service on July 29, 1866. Heitman, *Register,* 1: 953.

38. The tarantula is a large, hairy spider common in the Southwestern United States and Central America. Folklore attributes powers of death and other ills to its bite, but though painful, it is no more life threatening that that of most other spiders.

39. Boca Chica was at one time one of the two major outlets of the Rio Grande to the Gulf of Mexico. This opening formed the south end of Brazos Island, but was only about three feet deep during the time of the Mexican War and could be forded by wading. At the latter stages of the war, a pontoon bridge was built across Boca Chica. Boca Chica has now silted over.

40. George B. McClellan described how the soldiers camping on Brazos Island obtained drinking water:

> The water which we drink is obtained by digging a hole large enough to contain a barrel. In it is placed a bottomless barrel in which the water collects. You must dig until you find water, then "work-in" the barrel until it is well down. This water is very bad. It is brackish and unhealthy. William Starr Myers, *The Mexican War Diary of George B.McClellan* (Princeton, N.J.: Princeton University Press, 1917), 9.

41. The mouth of the Rio Grande was described by Samuel Ryan Curtis on July 31, 1846:

> On this side there are no buildings except two or three rough shantees made of planks and wrecks of steam boats which serve the officers as quarters....The houses [in Mexico] are about six to eight feet high with roof made of straw.... I went into the gardens where I found nothing but a luxuriant growth of pumpkin vines and melon vines...dogs and chickens and calves were the dominant animals...I found one of the buildings much better than the rest. It belonged to the pilot. It was made as most of the rancho buildings were said to be. Wood and mud walls about 8 feet high and covered with a high thatched roof. The floor was earth but clean sweeped.

"Diary of Samuel Ryan Curtis", Bancroft Library, Univ. of California, Berkley. The few Mexican buildings described by Curtis would form the nucleus of the booming town of Bagdad, to be built by the cotton trade during the American Civil War.

42. Schuyler Hamilton, an 1841 graduate of the United States Military Academy, was assigned to the 1st Infantry. He was cited for his actions during the capture of Monterrey, and for meritorious conduct in Central Mexico "...in the affair with the enemy at Mil Flores, Mexico" on August 13, 1847. He resigned from the service on March 31, 1855. Heitman, *Register*, 1: 494.

43. Capt. Robert Desha led an independent company of Alabama volunteers, illegally recruited for service by Gen. Edmund P. Gaines. Heitman, *Register*, 2: 19.

44. The *Neva* was a sidewheel river steamer of 141 tons owned by the United States Government, purchased to transport soldiers and supplies up the Rio Grande from Matamoros to Camargo. The Neva was one of the steamboats hurriedly purchased by the Quarter Master's Corps in the summer of 1846 to facilitate the logistics problems associated with the movement of the army within striking distance of

Monterrey. However, her hull was found, on close inspection, to be "so worm eaten as to be utterly useless." Risch, *Quarter Master*, 260, 265. The *American Flag* of July 1, 1846, reported this account on its general condition: "The Neva, After three companies of the 7th Infantry, with their baggage, had repaired on board this steamer for transportation, Gen. Taylor, ever mindful of the comfort and safety of his men, caused an inspection of her boilers to be made, and upon the intimation of their unfitness, ordered his men on terra firma, saying their lives were too precious to their country to be placed in jeopardy except in its defense. The steamer has gone below for repairs."

45. The officer mentioned was either Capt. Isaac F. Stockton or Capt. R. C. Stockton, both of the 1st Louisiana Volunteer Regiment. Heitman, *Register*, 2: 69.

46. Captain Sabin's Company of Tennessee Volunteers cannot be located. The group may have formed a portion of the volunteers illegally mustered for service by Gen. Edmund P. Gaines. The earliest reported Tennessee volunteers were members of the 1st Tennessee Volunteer Regiment, which landed on Brazos Island on June 24, 1846. John B. Robinson, *Reminiscences of a Campaign in Mexico, by a Member of the "Bloody-First"* (Nashville: John York & Co., 1849), 76.

47. The encampment sighted by Dilworth was probably Camp Belknap located on the north bank of the Rio Grande, where volunteer soldiers were settled and trained prior to their movement up the Rio Grande to Camargo. During its heyday, this camp was home to almost 8,000 American volunteers.

48. Lewis Dickenson was a 2d lieutenant of the Independent Company of Alabama Volunteers. Heitman, *Register*, 2: 49.

49. Gen. Mariano Arista (1820-55) was a noted Mexican cavalry officer born in San Luis Potosi and educated in the United States. He commanded the forces defeated by Gen. Zachary Taylor's army at the battles of Palo Alto and Resaca de la Palma. General Arista was the president of Mexico from 1851 to 1853. *Diccionario Porrua Historia, Biografia Y Geografia de Mexico*, (Mexico City: Editorial Porrua, 1965) 1: 139.

50. These cries were the litany of the sailor assigned to the anchor chains of a ship to cast the lead line. The line, used for sounding shallow water, was usually marked at intervals of one fathom for a deep draft ocean vessel to intervals of one foot for a shallow draft river steamer. The lead was slung ahead of the ship and the weight on the end of

the line would settle to the bottom as the ship approached. The sailor would draw up the line and read the marks, crying, "by the mark ten" to indicate for example a depth of ten feet. For a depth between two marks, the cry might be, "deep six," to indicate a depth between six and seven feet. Joachim Schult, *The Sailing Dictionary* (Frogmore, St. Albans: Granada Publishing Ltd., 1981), 150.

51. Gen. Persifor F. Smith was brigade commander of the Louisiana Volunteer Brigade, mustered illegally for service on or about May 15, 1846, by Gen. Edmund P. Gaines. The brigade consisted of the George Washington Regiment (1st Louisiana), commanded by Col. James B. Walton; the Louisiana Regiment (2d Louisiana), commanded by Col. James H. Dakin; the Andrew Jackson Regiment (3d Louisiana), commanded by Col. Samuel F. Marks; and the Montezuma Regiment (4th Louisiana), commanded by Col. Horatio Davis. Smith was a stern disciplinarian and forced the boys from New Orleans to perform manual labor in the hot sun. Samuel Curtis reported that

    > The Louisiana troops seem to have got dispirited because they were required to clean the ground of their encampments. It is said they gave their General (Genl Smith) the cognomen of Genl Chaparrel. A report circulated that he received five cents an acre for clearing land.

    The brigade was disbanded by order of Gen. Zachary Taylor, by July 1846 and the volunteers were transported on a return trip to Louisiana. Smith, however, was appointed by Congress to the rank of colonel to lead the Regiment of Mounted Riflemen. Smith and many other officers of the mounted regiment were selected from the ranks of civilian volunteers, causing great indignation among the regular officer corps. Many of the officers of the regular army, who had not received a promotion in ten years, suddenly found themselves outranked by the newly appointed regular officers. *American Flag,* July 19, 1846; "Diary of Samuel Ryan Curtis", Bancroft Library, Univ. of California, Berkeley, "entry for July 24, 1846."

52. Col. Samuel F. Marks commanded the 3d Regiment of Louisiana Volunteers. Heitman, *Register*, 2: 61.

53. The *Cincinnati* was a 276-ton sidewheel steamboat chartered by the United States for use as a lighter. She was reported as wrecked on the bar at Tampico in early 1847. Lytle and Holdcamper, *Merchant Steam Vessels*, 17; *American Flag*, February 3, 1847.

54. The Spanish word "vega" can be translated as a plain or a fertile plain.

55. General Arista ordered General Ampudia to cross the Rio Grande with the 1st Brigade at Longoreno about eight miles below Matamoros. This portion of the Rio Grande is still known locally as Arista's Crossing.

56. These *rancheros* were probably a part of the cavalry of about 400 irregular troops recruited and commanded by Gen. Antonio Canales. In the battle of May 8, 1846, Canales's cavalry formed the left wing of the Mexican line but was not active in the battle. On May 9, with two guns, Canales posted his rancheros on the extreme left of the Mexican defensive line, "a considerable distance from the Resaca" to guard a crossroad leading to the rear of the Mexican line. At sight of an American flanking attack, Canales "took flight." A young soldier with Canales was Juan Nepomuceno "Cheno" Cortina, who was later to become one of the leading and most controversial Mexican figures of the Texas-Mexico border in the Nineteenth Century. Luis Berlandier, the noted naturalist, also took up a musket to fight with Canales and his men in this action. Justin Smith, *The War With Mexico* (New York: Macmillan Co., 1919) 1: 171, 174.

57. The city of Matamoros was founded in 1774 by ten powerful ranching families living in Camargo, further up the Rio Grande. By 1796 the growing village was known as Nuestra Señora del Refugio de los Esteros (Our Lady of Refuge of the Lakes). In 1826 the city received its current name in honor of Padre Mariano Matamoros, who had been killed in the Mexican struggle for independence from Spain. Matamoros grew and became the official government port of entry for all trade goods entering northern Mexico. The actual port was Frontón, near Brazos Santiago, from where goods were carted overland to Matamoros. By 1844 Matamoros had been laid out in the Spanish style of squares, filled with many governmental buildings, markets, and a large and attractive church. The city had a population of 11,823 on the eve of the Mexican War. Milo Kearney and Anthony Knopp, *Boom and Bust: The Historical Cycles of Matamoros and Brownsville* (Austin: Eakin Press, 1991), 15-25.

58. There were two ferry crossings on the Rio Grande opposite Matamoros. Both ferrys were powered by a human operator on board the boat pulling on a rope that extended across the river. The lower crossing, named Paso Real, was adjacent to Fort Brown, and the upper, or Anacuitas Crossing, was stationed just below Fort Paredes, a Mexican fort northwest of Matamoros. A ferry propelled by a pull

rope can still be seen operating on the Rio Grande at Los Ebanos, below Sullivan City in Starr County.

59. Napoleon Jackson Tecumseh Dana graduated from the United States Military Academy in 1842 and was assigned to the 7th Infantry. He was cited for meritorious conduct during the battle of Cerro Gordo, Mexico. Dana resigned from the service in 1855, but returned in 1861 and rose to the rank of major general of volunteers by 1862. He retired from active duty on August 11, 1894. Heitman, *Register*, 1: 352.

60. Pitcairn Morrison joined the service in 1820 at the rank of 2d lieutenant and was assigned to the artillery. By 1822 he was transferred to the 4th Infantry and served in that regiment until his appointment as major of the 8th Infantry on September 26, 1847. He was cited for meritorious conduct at the battles of Palo Alto and Resaca de la Palma on May 8-9, 1846. He retired from the service on October 20, 1863. Heitman, *Register*, 1: 729.

61. George Gordon Meade reported the same difficulty with the mail service to Matamoros on this date:

> The papers by the last mail bring us the intelligence of the action of Congress, the President's proclamation, the rumor that thirty thousand men are to be sent here, and some say General Scott to command them. Unfortunately the mail rider from Point Isabel lost his mail yesterday, and it is said to be the most important mail ever sent to us, as it contains all the information in official documents. Parties have been sent to look for it and I trust may yet be recovered. George Gordon Meade, *The Life and Letters of George Gordon Meade* (New York: Charles Scribner's Sons, 1913), 1: 92.

June

1. The Tampico Regiment was considered to be one of the crack infantry regiments in the Mexican Army. The colors of the Tampico Regiment, as well as all of the other captured regimental flags, were brought to Washington by Lt. Col. Matthew Mountjoy Payne of the 4th Artillery, who had been wounded in the battles of May 8 and 9. Payne was received by Pres. James K. Polk, who wrote for his diary entry of July 18, 1846:

> Lieut. Col. Payne of the United States Army called...to exhibit to me several Mexican flags as the trophies of the victory of the 8th and 9th May on the Rio Grande. These flags were captured from the enemy in the battles on those days, and two of them had been perforated by balls in these battles. Col. Payne himself was in these battles and had been severely wounded. He walks now on his crutches.

Allan Nevins, *Polk: The Diary of a President* (London: Longmans, Green and Co., 1952), 126.

2. Gen. Antonio Canales, (1800?—1852?) was a lawyer born in Monterrey. He was one of the men who plotted to free northern Mexico from the central government and establish the independent Republic of the Rio Grande. His forces, which enlisted the services of many Texans, were defeated on the Rio Grande in 1839. The Texans under Canales felt that they had been betrayed by his actions and swore to seek revenge. Canales and his force of irregulars aided in the capture of the Texans that invaded Mier on December 25, 1842, in the incident that came to be known as the Mier Expedition. During the Mexican War, Canales sided with Mexico and established a large force of rancheros that fought a guerrilla war in northern Mexico against United States forces. His hit-and-run battle tactics against the Americans earned him the name "Chaparral Fox" by his adversaries. With the help of the forces of Gen. Jose Urrea, Canales and other guerrilla leaders were able to completely interdict all supply and communications lines to Taylor's forces in Saltillo for more than two months during the early part of 1847. After the war, Canales became governor of the State of Tamaulipas in 1851. Gustav Dreisel gave this eyewitness description of him: "Canales, a little man of brown complexion, had eyes as false as those of a mustang." *Dicconario Porrua* pg. 345; Max Freund, *Gustav Dresel's Houston Journal* (Austin: Univ. of Texas Press, 1954), 101.
3. William Wallace Smith Bliss graduated from the United States Military Academy in 1833 and was assigned to the 4th Infantry. He rose to the rank of captain by July 1846 and became, at that time, adjutant to Gen. Zachary Taylor. He was cited for gallantry and meritorious conduct at the battles of Palo Alto, Resaca de la Palma, and Buena Vista. He died on August 5, 1853. Heitman, *Register*, 1: 225.
4. Zebulon Montgomery Pike Inge graduated from the United States Military Academy in 1838 and was assigned to the 2d Dragoons. He

was killed in action on May 9, 1846, at the battle of Resaca de la Palma. Heitman, *Register,* 1: 562.

5. Richard E. Cochrane joined the service in 1838 at the rank of 2d lieutenant and was assigned to the 4th Infantry. He was killed in action on May 9, 1846, at the battle of Resaca de la Palma. Heitman, *Register.* 1: 313.

6. In 1967, while excavating for the development of a new housing subdivision in northern Brownsville, workers unearthed a mass grave of Mexican soldiers. A team of archeologists from the University of Texas at Austin, led by Dr. Thomas Hester, examined the site. The skeletons, or partial skeletons, of thirty-two Mexican soldiers were excavated from this site. The main artifacts found were shirt and trouser buttons, canteens, buckles, and musket balls "some found in what were evidently lethal locales." A final report on the excavations and subsequent analyses was never prepared. "An Exploration of a Common Legacy: A Conference on Border Architecture," *Proceedings* (Austin: Texas Historical Commission, 1978), 71.

7. George Henry Thomas graduated from the United States Military Academy in 1840 and was assigned to the 3d Artillery. He served in the artillery throughout the Mexican War and was cited for gallant and meritorious conduct for his actions during the attack on Monterrey and the battle of Buena Vista. Thomas rose to the rank of major general in the Union Army and was tendered the thanks of Congress by a resolution of March 3, 1865, "That the thanks of Congress are due, and are hereby tendered, to Maj. Gen. George H. Thomas and the officers and soldiers under his command for their skill and dauntless courage, by which the rebel army under Gen. Hood was signally defeated and driven from the State of Tennessee." He died on March 28, 1870. Heitman, *Register,* 1: 953.

8. Bushrod Rust Johnson graduated from the United States Military Academy in 1840 and was assigned to the 3d Infantry. He resigned from the service on October 22, 1847. During the War for Southern Independence, Johnson rose to the rank of major general in the CSA Army. He died on September 7, 1880. Heitman, *Register,* 1: 574.

9. Braxton Bragg graduated from the United States Military Academy in 1837 and was assigned to the 3d Artillery. He was cited for gallantry and distinguished conduct for his actions in the defense of Fort Brown, the capture of Monterrey, and the battle of Buena Vista. He resigned his commission on 3 January 1856, and rose to the rank of

general in the CSA Army during the War for Southern Independence. He died on September 27, 1876. Heitman, *Register,* 1: 240.

10. Capt. John T. Price's company of Texas Rangers was sent to escort four companies of the 1st Infantry and a section of Braxton Bragg's battery on the expedition to Reynosa. *American Flag,* June 6, 1846.

11. The Rangers later came to be called "los diablos Tejanos" or the Texas Devils because of their violence towards the Mexicans. Taylor felt that the Texans killed unnecessarily and wrote that "some disgraceful atrocities have been perpetrated by them." Walter Prescott Webb,*The Texas Rangers* (Austin: UT Press, 1982) 119; K. Jack Bauer, *General Zachary Taylor: Soldier, Planter, Statesman of the Old Southwest* (Baton Rouge: LSU Press, 1985), 185.

12. Granville Owen Haller joined the 4th Infantry in 1839 at the rank of 2d lieutenant. He was cited for gallantry and meritorious conduct for his actions at the battle of Molino del Rey and the capture of Chapultepec Castle. He retired from the service in 1882. Heitman, *Register,* 1: 491.

13. George H. Crosman graduated from the United States Military Academy in 1823 and was assigned to the 3d Infantry. By 1830, he had transferred to the Quarter Master Corps and served throughout the Mexican War in that capacity. He was cited for meritorious conduct at the battle of Palo Alto. Crosman rose to the rank of major general in the Union Army, and retired from the service in 1866. Heitman, *Register,* 1: 340.

14. The gourd canteen was a favorite way to carry water for soldiers of both armies. Soldiers disliked the metal canteen because the water inside heated up during the day. The only other alternative was a canteen constructed of "India rubber" that flavored the water with an unpleasant taste. The gourd, shaped like a figure eight, held about a quart of water in a porous, remarkably strong container that kept the water cool and imparted no taste. A strap was tied around the narrow center and could be carried over the shoulder or on the pommel of a saddle. The gourds are still grown in Mexico for the same purpose and can be found in the United States, grown to make bird houses.

15. Reynosa, a city with a present population of about half a million people, lies about sixty miles above Matamoros on the Rio Grande. In 1846, Meade described Reynosa as

> A small place, not having at present over six hundred inhabitants, and containing evidence of magnificent designs most meagrely executed. The town is laid out in squares upon a hill some fifty feet high, consisting of a rotten limestone, which material is used in constructing the houses. These, as in all their towns, are only one story and with square roofs. The walls are made nearly two feet thick, of this spongy limestone, and put together in immense blocks, with a cement of very inferior quality, made from the limestone. About one-half the houses are only half built; of the remainder, a large proportion are tumbling to pieces; so, in fact, though a town of recent date, one would suppose it was a century old from its apparently dilapidated state.

Meade, *Life*, 107.

16. Meade reported that General Canales and his rancheros were in the neighborhood of Reynosa plundering the countryside. He notes that "a deputation of the principal citizens of Reynosa waited on the General [Taylor] to ask his protection, inasmuch as the Mexican Government had deserted them, and they were in fear of the Indians. As soon as they returned home, Canales seized them and threw them into prison." Meade, *Life*, 98.

17. An alcalde is the leader of the municipal government in a Mexican city or village, and corresponds to the position of mayor in an American city, but has more power than his American counterpart.

18. A simoon is a hot suffocating wind in Africa or Arabia.

19. Pedro de Ampudia was born in 1805 in Havana, Cuba. He came to Mexico in 1821 and fought against the Spanish, participating in the assault on the San Juan de Ulloa Castle at Vera Cruz. After Santa Anna deposed Bustamente as president in 1840, Ampudia became a general in the army. He participated with Gen. Adrian Woll in an invasion of Texas in 1842 and led the troops that captured Col. William S. Fisher and his Texans at Mier, Mexico, on December 26, 1842. Shifted to southern Mexico, he fought against separatist forces in the Yucatan, commanding the siege of Campeche. During the war with the United States, Ampudia commanded the defenses of the city of Monterrey. After the fall of that city to the Americans, he proceeded to San Luis Potosí, where he was appointed quarter master general of the forces raised by Santa Anna for the defense of Mexico. Ampudia fought in the battle of Buena Vista. After the war, he was active in politics, be-

coming governor of the state of Nuevo León in 1854. He died in 1868. *Diccionario,* 1: 101.

20. Gen. Francisco Mejia was the commander of the Mexican army stationed at Matamoros when Taylor's army arrived opposite that city in late March 1846.

21. Linares is a Mexican town in the State of Nuevo Leon about eighty miles southeast of Monterrey.

22. Ben McCulloch's company of Texas Rangers arrived in Reynosa about June 21, 1846, after a scout of the road from Matamoros to Linares and a detour over to the Monterrey-Reynosa road. Samuel Reid of the company reported the town was alive with rumors of attack from Mexican Rancheros led either by Antonio Canales or by Juan Seguín. Colonel Wilson was perturbed by the many rumors, mostly designed for his benefit and "for some time previous to our arrival, the colonel had his command on double duty, fearful from the information he daily received from the friendly town-people." This is the possible reason that Dilworth had been ordered to stand guard every third night. Samuel Reid, *The Scouting Expeditions of McCulloch's Rangers* (Austin: Steck Co., 1935), 52-53.

23. William Brooke Johns graduated from the United States Military Academy in 1840 and was assigned to the 8th Infantry. He was cited for gallantry and meritorious conduct for his actions at the battle of Cerro Gordo and was dropped from the rolls of the service on April 11, 1861. Heitman, *Register,* 1: 574.

24. Mexicans celebrated the week from June 18 to 25 as the Feast of St. John. Helen Chapman reported from Matamoros on June 25, 1848, that

    > Yesterday was the closing day of the Festival of St. John and the custom is for everybody that can procure anything in the form of a horse to ride for very life through the streets. These Mexicans have a wild look on horseback. They carry a very loose rein, use their spurs constantly, and put their animals to their utmost speed. I cannot conceive what natural connection there is between St. John and this break-neck cantering . . .

    Samuel Reid observed the same custom celebrated in the streets of Reynosa on June 25, 1846,

    > Whooping and yelling like Indians, they dash through the streets in large parties, charging upon and riding down everything that

> impedes their progress. Single horsemen sometimes meet in full career, and as it is disgraceful to give the road on such occasions, they ride directly upon one another, and the consequence is, that the weakest horse or the most unskillful rider is dashed to the ground, while the victor rides on in triumph.

Reynosa horsemen attempted to ride down McCulloch's Rangers in the same feat of daring but found to their rude shock that their wiry mustangs were no match for the big American thoroughbreds ridden by the Rangers. The Mexicans exclaimed in praise, "los cavallos Americanos son mucho bueno...."

Col. Wilson would not allow the McCulloch Rangers to occupy any Mexican housing in Reynosa, stating that, " My orders are positive, I cannot suffer any Mexican domiciles to be encroached upon...the quarters of a soldier in the time of war, is the field." Thus said, Wilson walked into his quarters, a comfortable stone house. The almost daily deluge of rain made camping outdoors miserable, and finally when a mutiny was imminent, Wilson recanted and furnished the Rangers shelter in an abandoned cotton gin shed. Caleb Coker, ed., *The News From Brownsville* (Austin: Texas State Historical Association, 1992) 53-54; Reid, *McCulloch's Rangers*, 54-60.

JULY

1. The *Frontier* was a sidewheel river steamboat of 109 tons, built in Louisville, Kentucky in 1843. Pat Kelley, *River of Lost Dreams* (Lincoln: University of Nebraska Press, 1987), 109. The *American Flag* of June 6, 1846, a newpaper published in Matamoros, reported the following:

> Capt. Thomas P. Clark, well known and highly appreciated on the Mississippi river as an experienced steam-boatman, has brought into service a light draft boat, which he has appropriately named the "Frontier." He designs running her regularly between Matamoros and Point Isabel, and possessing fine accommodations and great speed, she will afford superior facilities for travel and communication between these points. His prices, $10 for cabin and $3 for deck passengers, are as low as could be expected, considering the expense he incurs. The *Frontier* is an independent boat, not being regularly enlisted in government service, therefore we trust he will receive sufficient patronage to

> compensate him for the risk he incurs and the enterprise he exhibits. Travelers will remember the "Frontier."

The *Frontier* did not last long on the turbulent Texas coast. By July 19, 1846, Reid reported

> On nearing the mouth of the river [Rio Grande], she [*Frontier*] stuck on the bar in the midst of the breakers....The gale increasing, the sea made a complete breach over her, and it was feared that she would soon become a wreck....It was left for morning to tell the tale of her wreck, for at daylight she went to pieces.

Reid, *The Scouting Expeditions of McCulloch's Texas Rangers*, 18-19.

2. Seams of lignite coal were reported near the town of Revilla (Guerrero), now partially submerged by Falcon Lake, which is above Roma, Texas, on the Rio Grande. Emory reported that "outcrops of it [lignite coal], however, are said to be found in the neighborhood of Roma, some ten miles above the mouth of the Rio San Juan." The most considerable amounts of lignite coal are found in the vicinity of Eagle Pass, Texas, and explains why the sister city of Eagle Pass across the Rio Grande is named Piedras Negras. William H. Emory, *Report on the United States Boundary Survey* (Austin: Texas State Historical Assn., 1987), Part 2: 35.

3. That illustrous Texan, Ben McCulloch, led a spy company in Taylor's army during the Mexican War. He conducted a daring reconnaissance of the Mexican Army on the eve of the battle of Buena Vista by entering their camps disguised as a Mexican. His accurate assessment of Mexican strength was one of the deciding factors in Taylor's decision to pull the American Army back from its position at Agua Nueva to Angostura Pass. After the Mexican War, McCulloch traveled to California and while there served a term as sheriff of Sacramento County. He returned to Texas and was appointed United States marshal by Pres. Franklin Pierce. McCulloch was killed at the battle of Elk Horn Tavern in northern Arkansas on March 7, 1862, while leading Confederate forces from the states of Arkansas, Louisiana, and Texas. His body was returned to Texas and he was buried with military honors in the State Cemetery at Austin. Walter P. Webb, ed, *Handbook of Texas* (Austin: Texas State Historical Assn., 1952), 2: 106.

4. George Wilkins Kendall holds the distinction of being one of the first American war correspondents. Kendall and F. A. Lumsden founded the New Orleans *Picayune* in 1837, to furnish "penny press" news to an eager American public. Unlike their European brothers and sisters,

most Americans had received enough education to at least read and write from the one-room school houses that sprang up in every community. Newly invented steam presses made newspapers cheap and plentiful for this large market of readers. With the advent of the Mexican War, readers clamored for up-to-date news, and Kendall took to the field to supply this need. He went with the American Army into northern Mexico to gather the news and organized a system of pony express riders to rapidly communicate with his many readers. Kendall always tried to be where action was occurring, and naturally followed the Texas Rangers on their many scouts into northern Mexico. Thomas William Reilly, "American Reporters and the Mexican War," Ph. D. Diss., University of Minnesota, 1975, 52-84.

5. The *Aid* was a sidewheel shallow draft steamboat of 137 tons, built in Cincinnati, Ohio, in 1843. It was chartered by the United States government for use on the Rio Grande from its owner, Charles Stillman, a famous Matamoros and Brownsville entrepreneur. Kelley, *River of Lost Dreams*, 107.

6. William Whistler joined the service as a 2d lieutenant in the 1st Infantry in 1801. He rose to the rank of colonel of the 4th Infantry by 1845 and retired from the service on October 9, 1861. Lieutenant Dana reported on April 17, 1846, from the camp opposite Matamoros:

   > Poor old Colonel Whistler is in arrest again and they say that this time he will be dismissed. He was drunk on the morning when the Mexicans said that they would open their batteries. I don't know what the old lady will do about that. She will have to economize in real earnest if the colonel is obliged to leave the service.

   Dana's entry for April 23, 1846, reported that

   > Colonel Whistler, I understand, leaves today. Poor old man, he is very crestfallen. If they really intend to try him, he had better resign at once and save himself from disgrace, for if he is tried he is probably a gone coon.

   Whistler was removed from command of the 4th Infantry. Heitman, *Register*, 1: 1026; Dana, *Monterrey is Ours!*, 45, 51.

7. The *American Flag* of Aug. 14, 1846, presented the case for the regular officers who had been passed over by Congress and Pres. James K. Polk in appointments to the new Regiment of Mounted Rifles:

> It was naturally supposed, when Congress authorised...the appointment of new officers, particularly those of the higher grades, the President would eagerly avail himself of the opportunity to promote the gallant men, for whose late brilliant exploits he professes to be so very grateful, and some who have grown grey in the service of their country.... The consequence has been, that, superciliously passing by the intrepid defenders of Fort Brown, and the conquerors of the Mexicans on the bloody and glorious fields of Palo Alto and Resaca de la Palma, the President has officered the new regiment with individuals, who, with three or four exceptions, have never "fleshed their maiden swords" even in a holyday parade; mere "carpet knights," who ought at least to have won their spurs before they put them on.
>
> And why were not the subalterns selected from the ranks, instead of searching for them among gentlemen who were out of harm's way, while they were baring their breast to the foe? The injustice of the course pursued in making these appointments is rendered more flagrant by the fact that several of the new officers were formerly pupils at West Point, but did not graduate, either from incapacity, or something worse, and yet they now rank higher than their classmates, who after graduating, joined the army and have ever since been performing their duty.

8. The *J. E. Roberts* was a sidewheel river steamboat of 118 tons, built in Grave Neck, Virginia, in 1844. She was owned by the United States government and used for the movement of soldiers and supplies from the mouth of the Rio Grande to Camargo, Mexico. Kelley, River, 110; Risch, *Quarter Master*, 261.

9. William Chapman graduated from the United States Military Academy in 1827 and was assigned to the 5th Infantry. He rose to the rank of brevet major for gallantry and meritorious conduct at the battles of Contreras and Churubusco, and was later promoted to the rank of brevet lieutenant-colonel for gallantry at the battle of Molina del Rey. He rose to the rank of colonel in the Union Army for meritorious conduct at the battle of Bull Run. Chapman died on December 17, 1887. Heitman, *Register*, 1: 296.

10. Thomas Staniford joined the service in 1812 at the rank of ensign and was assigned to the 11th Infantry. He rose to the rank of major in the 5th Infantry by 1845 and was cited for meritorious conduct at the battles of Palo Alto and Resaca de la Palma. He was promoted to the rank of lieutenant-colonel of the 8th Infantry on June 29, 1846, and was

cited again for his actions during the capture of Monterrey. He died on February 3, 1855. Heitman, *Register,* 1: 915.

11. David Emanuel Twiggs joined the service at the rank of captain in 1812. He rose to the rank of brigadier general by June 30, 1846. He was cited for gallantry and meritorious conduct for his actions in the capture of Monterrey and was voted a sword by Congress on March 2, 1847, "in testimony of the high sense entertained by Congress of his gallantry and good conduct in storming Monterey." He was dismissed from the service in March 1861 and rose to the rank of major general CSA. He died July 15, 1862. Sgt. James Mullan, Jr., an enlisted man serving in Twigg's division just prior to the attack on Monterrey, remembered his blustery qualities. His journal entry of September 15, 1846, stated, "...Twiggs is a horse he can Curse a man right out of his boots." Heitman, *Register,* 1: 976; The Justin Smith Transcripts, Latin American Collection, University of Texas Library, Austin, Texas.

12. Stephen Watts Kearny joined the service at the rank of first lieutentant in the 13th Infantry in 1812. He rose to the rank of brigadier general by June 30, 1846. He was cited for gallantry and meritorious conduct in New Mexico and California. Kearny died on October 31, 1848. Heitman, *Register,* 1: 586.

AUGUST

1. Joseph Stewart graduated from the United States Military Academy in 1842 and served in the 3d Artillery during the Mexican War. He retired from the service on August 25, 1879. Heitman, *Register,* 1: 925.

2. San Fernando was a small Mexican village about ninety miles southwest of Matamoros.

3. The correct name was probably Rancho Los Morillos, located about three leagues from Reynosa.

4. The city of Reynosa was founded in 1749 on the banks of the Rio Grande about sixty miles west of Matamoros. The original site of the city, now known as Reynosa Veijo (Old Reynosa), was on low ground and prone to frequent flooding. To alleviate this problem, Reynosa was moved to its present location on a limestone bluff. At the time of the Mexican War, a small settlement existed at Reynosa Veijo.

5. Camargo is a Mexican town situated on the east bank of the Rio San Juan about four miles above the junction of that river with the Rio Grande. Camargo is about 140 miles from Matamoros as the crow flies but is at least twice that far for someone travelling by boat along the Rio Grande. The town consisted of about 2,000 inhabitants in early 1846, but many fled after the disastrous overflow of the Rio San Juan in June 1846 that destroyed a large portion of the town. Camargo became a vast supply depot during the Mexican War, and served nominally as the head of navigation on the Rio Grande. From this town, the American army assembled for the march overland to Monterrey about 100 miles southwest. Camps for American soldiers lined the Rio San Juan for many miles on both sides of Camargo. Sickness swept the American camps in Camargo, then wholesale death. Regimental bands so often struck up the chords of the death march in funeral services at Camargo that the mockingbirds of that area began to whistle that dolorous refrain. An American volunteer referred to Camargo as "a yawning grave," and it is estimated that about 1,500 unmarked American graves line the banks of the Rio San Juan.
At Camargo and in fact along the lower Rio Grande it was a common sight to see nude Mexican women bathing in the river. Lieutenant Dana reported that

> Many women used to go bathing in the river before and among the men, and many went down especially to look at them. Among others that beast [Nevil] Hopson [see August n.18] used to spend half the day at the river bank....
> Those sights of naked women have not been seen, I believe, since we left Camargo....Poor Terrett, he was a man of a troublesome degree of modesty, and at Reynosa whilst he was in bathing once a couple of women came down and sat on the bank close to him, looking at him with perfect innocence. He was in a great quandry how to get out, and they kept the poor fellow in a long time. At last they stripped right off and went in alongside of him. Terrett left the place in perfect disgust and towering indignation, swearing that Mexican women were no better than beasts nor half so modest and that he would never go near the river again by daylight whilst he was in Mexico.
> Captain [Electus] Backus tells a story: whilst he was riding near the river at Reynosa one day, a woman came up to him out of the water, perfectly stark naked, stood and talked with him and had not even the decency to put her hand before it...

Dana, *Monterrey is Ours!*, 144.

6. The Rio San Juan is a small river that heads up near Saltillo, passes through Monterrey, where it is known locally as the Santa Catarina, and flowing in a generally northeasterly direction from there enters the Rio Grande below Rio Grande City, Texas.

7. The revised United States Army Regulations for 1861, articles 515-523, discuss the layout of a camp for a company of infantry. The soldiers' tents are to be laid out in two lines with a company street between the two rows. At the end of the tent rows and perpendicular to the company street is the color line, so called because the company colors are often displayed on this line. Soldiers' muskets are stacked along this line. Soldiers assemble along this line in formation with muskets shouldered in response to the long roll of the drum, a call to arms.

8. William Jenkins Worth joined the service as a lieutenant of the 23d Infantry in 1813. He rose to the rank of major general during the Mexican War. He was cited for his gallantry and distinguished conduct at the battle of Chippewa, the battle of Niagara, for distinguished service as commander of the forces in the war against the Florida Indians, and for his meritorious service in the capture of Monterrey. Worth was voted a sword by Congress on March 2, 1847, "in testimony of the high sense entertained in his gallant and good conduct in the storming of Monterey, Mexico." He died on May 7, 1849. Heitman, *Register,* 1: 1061.

9. Thomas Childs graduated from the United States Military Academy in 1814 and was assigned to the 1st Artillery. He rose to the rank of brigadier general by October, 1847. During the Mexican War he was cited for gallant conduct during the battles of Palo Alto and Resaca de la Palma, and meritorious conduct in the defense of Puebla, Mexico. Childs died on October 8, 1853. Heitman, *Register,* 1: 299.

10. James Duncan was a graduate of the United States Military Academy in 1834 and assigned to the 2d Artillery. He was cited for gallant conduct at the battle of Palo Alto and highly distinguished service during the battle of Resaca de la Palma and the capture of Monterrey. Duncan died at the rank of colonel on July 3, 1849. Heitman, *Register,* 1: 387.

11. Richard B. Screven graduated from the United States Military Academy in 1825 and was assigned to the 2d Infantry in 1829. He was promoted to the rank of captain in 1838, serving in the 8th Infantry. For gallantry and meritorious conduct in the battle of Monterrey, he was promoted to the rank of brevet major on September 23, 1846, and finally rose to the rank of lieutenant-colonel for gallantry and meri-

torious conduct at the battle of Molina del Rey on September 8, 1847. He died on May 15, 1851. Heitman, *Register*, 1: 870.

12. Maj. Thomas Staniford, see July n.10.

13. William W. Lear joined the army at the rank of private in 1812. By the time of the Mexican War he had risen to the rank of major of the 3d Infantry. He died October 31, 1846, of wounds received on September 21, 1846, during the capture of Monterrey. Lieutenant Dana reported on October 13 that "Major Lear is still doing well. A bullet passed in at his mouth, crushed the bones of the face, and came out at the ear." Heitman, *Register*, 1: 621; Dana, *Monterrey is Ours!*, 145.

14. John Garland joined the service in 1813 at the rank of lieutenant in the 35th Infantry. By the time of the Mexican War, he held the rank of lieutenant-colonel in the 4th Infantry. He was cited for gallant conduct at the battles of Palo Alto and Resaca de la Palma, and for gallant and meritorious conduct at the battles of Contreras and Churubusco. He died on June 5, 1861, at the rank of colonel. Heitman, *Register*, 1: 447.

15. The 1st Texas Foot Riflemen was a regiment mustered into Federal service on July 7, 1846, and mustered out on August 4, 1846. The Texans had been assembled at Camargo in preparation for the attack on Monterrey when it was realized that their term of enlistment would quite likely expire in the field before they could be of any value to Taylor's army. General Taylor gave the Texans the option of enlisting for a year or being mustered out of service. Their colonel, Albert Sidney Johnston, mounted a stump and delivered an impassioned harangue to the Texans, begging them to re-enlist for at least a year more to bring the war to its completion. But good-natured Sidney Johnston, who often offered this example to his friends as evidence of what a poor public speaker he was, could only sway the vote of one man. The entire regiment was disbanded. Spurlin, *Veterans*, 7; William P. Johnston, *The Life of Albert Sidney Johnston* (New York: D. Appleton and Co., 1878), 136.

16. James F. Harrison was a 2d lieutenant in the 1st Ohio Volunteer Regiment. Heitman, *Register*, 2: 54.

17. In a meeting on May 19, 1846, Pres. James K. Polk discussed with Bishop John Hughes of New York how the government might counter the prejudices of the Catholic priests in Mexico. Polk felt that the idea was widely circulated in Mexico that "our object was to overthrow their religion and rob their churches, and that if they believed this

they would make a desperate resistance to our army in the present war." Polk suggested to the bishop that Spanish-speaking priests from the United States be sent to accompany the army in Mexico. Bishop Hughes agreed to the idea, and Rev. John McElroy and Rev. Antony Rey were dispatched to Mexico. Father Rey followed the army to Camargo and on to Monterrey where he conducted several services in the great cathedral there. Father Rey was murdered by bandits near the town of Marin on January 15, 1847. While passing near the village, robbers attacked his unarmed party, killing his servant. The clerical habit worn by the priest caused the bandits to halt further violence, but Father Rey was finally killed on the command of a bandit leader, who wished to leave no witnesses to the earlier crime. The populace of Marin, in tears of indignation and regret, received the body and interred it near the village. Father McElroy remained at his post in Matamoros until mid-1847 when ill health forced his return to the United States. Nevins, *Polk*, 96; K. Jack Bauer, *The Mexican War 1846-48*, 85; Sister Blanche Marie McEniry, *American Catholics in the War with Mexico* (Washington: Catholic University, 1932), 66.

18. The court-martial for Nevil Hopson convened at Camargo on August 22, 1846. The first specification was conduct unbecoming an officer and a gentleman. Hopson was charged with visiting the drinking establishments in Camargo while officially on sick leave and "close familiarity with a drunken Mexican, to all appearance of the lowest class." It was further charged that while in a state of intoxication he did "enter a house, the residence of a Mexican family in the plaza at Camargo, Mexico,...and did there publicly expose himself by dancing upon the floor himself, he having at or about the same time plainly visible, a bottle thrust into the breast of his coat or shirt." Several other charges were lodged against Hopson, all involving public intoxication and drinking. The court found Hopson guilty and sentenced him to be dismissed from the service. Orders 103, Orders of General Zachary Taylor to the Army of Occupation in the Mexican War, 1845-47, National Archives and Records Service.

19. A court-martial was convened and charges of desertion were lodged against Pvts. Samuel Reynolds, Henry Snower, Levi Swan, James Eagan, Mac Goldsbury, and Robert Brady. Sgt. William Bewers was charged with drunkenness, Pvt. James Hill with disobedience of orders, and Pvt. John Cramshire with mutinous conduct. All were found guilty, and a typical sentence was "to have fifty lashes on his bare back well laid on with a raw hide, to forfeit all pay and allowances that are or may be due him, except the just-debts due the sutler and the laun-

dress, to have the letter D one and a half inches long indelibly marked on his left hip, and to be drummed out of the service." These charges, however, were remitted due to "the present circumstances." Orders 101, Taylor Orders.

20. On August 17, 1846, Gen. Taylor staged the largest review of American regulars at Camargo that had been seen in the army since the time of the War of 1812. The line of troops extended more that three-fourths of a mile and included thirty-four companies of men, mounted dragoons, and two batteries of field artillery. The volunteers in camp watched with respect as the American Eagle screamed a warning to its enemies on the plains of Mexico.

21. Bennet Riley joined the service at the rank of ensign in 1813. By the time of the Mexican War, he had risen to the rank of lieutenant-colonel of the 2d Infantry. He was cited for gallant and meritorious conduct at the battle of Cerro Gordo, and for gallant conduct at the battle of Contreras. He died on June 9, 1853, at the rank of colonel. Heitman, *Register,* 1: 831.

22. Randolph Ridgely graduated from the United States Military Academy in 1837 and was assigned to the 3d Artillery. He was cited for gallantry and distinguished conduct at the battles of Palo Alto and Resaca de la Palma. Ridgeley was killed on a fall from his horse in Monterrey, on October 27, 1846. The daring Ridgely was one of the most popular men in the army, and his sudden death was a shock to all. The famous Kentucky orator Thomas F. Marshall commented, "As well might one expect to hear of an eagle dying from the fall of his wings as to hear of Randolph Ridgeley's dying from the fall of his horse." Heitman, *Register,* 1: 830; Joseph E. Chance, *The Mexican War Diary of Captain Franklin Smith* (Jackson: University Press of Mississippi, 1991), 155.

23. The Second Regiment of Texas Mounted Volunteers, known as the East Texas Rangers, was led by Col. George T. Wood. The regiment fought with great bravery at Monterrey and gained so much public approval for its leader that Wood was elected as the second governor of the state of Texas in 1847. Spurlin, *Texas Veterans,* 34.

24. Saltillo, the capital of the state of Coahuila, was founded by Capt. Alberto del Canto in 1575. The city, known as Leona Vicario at one time, is an important center for agriculture and ranching. The name is derived from the Spanish word "salto" for waterfall to describe the little waterfall from a spring which once flowed in the center of the city. Saltillo lies in the mountains about fifty-five miles southwest of

Monterrey, through a pass rimmed by rugged mountains. *Diccionario Porrua*, 1842.

25. Clouds of caliche dust, stirred up by wagon wheels, horses' hooves, and the tramping of marching feet, hung over the town of Camargo. Franklin Smith, a volunteer at Camargo and no admirer of Gen. Robert Patterson, reported

> The General [Robert Patterson] issued an order that no wagons or horsemen should pass the street facing his palace door...Twenty times a day he and his orderly and the sentry on his pavement have been thrown into spasms at ignorant teamsters and horsemen endeavoring to pass.
> —He has consequently lost a great deal of sleep, had to swallow much unmilitary dust, and he's doubtless had a fit of indigestion. ...Col. [Charles] May and Lieutenant [Forbes] Britton affecting not to understand the order or to forget it gallop past the palace door a dozen times a day with lightning speed and raising a devil of a dust lost in the clouds of their own creation before the sentinel has time to call a halt. Now to send Britton to the guardhouse would be an easy matter but to imprison the gallant May now the darling son of America and dear to all hearts for galloping down a public street in a town which he helped to conquer must give the Comdg. Genl. pause.

Joseph E. Chance, *The Mexican War Diary of Captain Franklin Smith* (Jackson: Univ. Press of Mississippi, 1991), 70-1.

26. The order issued by General Taylor cannot be found, but it is probably the same as the one issued on October 14, 1846, by Maj. Gen. Robert Patterson, who was military governor of Camargo and the military installations on the Rio Grande. This order read, in part,

> No person not attached to the Army will be received as a passenger on board said boats, without the written permission of the Commanding Officer of one of the Mil. Posts on the river, or a Commissioned Officer of the Qr Mr. Dept.

General Orders, vol. 43, Justin Smith Transcripts, University of Library, Austin, Texas. The purpose of this order was to keep gamblers, prostitutes, and other general troublemakers from gaining access to the many soldiers in the camps at Camargo. The Army had learned from bitter experience in Matamoros what could happen to a city when flooded by persons of this caliber from the United States looking for "easy money." The order further banned the importation of "all intoxicating liquors, whether spiritous, vinous, or fermented." Patterson had his hands full enforcing this last order, and details of many of his trials and tribulations can by found in Chance, *Mexican War Diary of Captain Franklin Smith.*

27. Elias Kent Kane was a graduate of the United States Military Academy in 1841 and was assigned to the 2d Dragoons. He died on July 9, 1853, at the rank of captain. Heitman, *Register,* 1: 585.

28. Gen. Thomas Hamer, an Ohio politician, commanded the brigade of Ohio volunteers. He appointed U. S. Grant to the United States Military Academy, and Grant would write of him in later years:

> I have said before that Hamer was one of the ablest men Ohio ever produced. At that time [1846] he was in the prime of life, being less than fifty years of age, and possessed an admirable physique, promising long life. But he was taken sick before Monterrey, and died within a few days. I have always believed that had his life been spared, he would have been President of the United States during the term filled by President Pierce. Long, *Grant,* 48.

29. The "New Camargo" referred to by Dilworth is known locally as "Villanueva." The deserted village of stone and adobe buildings is located about two miles southwest of Camargo on a hill above the floodplain of the Rio San Juan and on the west side of that river.

30. José María Jesús Carbajal was born in San Antonio, Texas, and sided with the Texas Revolution, being elected to the Convention of 1836 as a delegate from Bexar. During the Mexican War, he led a band of Mexican rancheros, quartered around San Fernando, that fought a guerrilla war against the American Army. Between 1850 and 1853, he became associated with several raids from Texas into Mexico that came to be known as the Merchant's War. He served as governor of the state of Tamaulipas in 1865, and died in Soto la Marina in 1874. Teresa Viele offered this description of Carbajal:

> He was a small man, with a dark complexion and an eagle eye, the beauty of his excessively ugly face-like a Scotch terrier-consisting of this very ugliness combined with an expression of great intelligence. The first time I saw him, I was on horseback, riding across the chapparal to the ranche...When we met Caravajal, I knew him in an instant, by the stylish way in which he wore his black felt sombrero, by the silver-mounted pistols in his belt, and by the pure English accent of his salutation.

Webb, *Handbook of Texas,* 1: 294; Viele, *Following the Drum,* 193.

31. On August 16, 1846, Santa Anna reentered Mexico from exile in Cuba, and with the help of powerful friends, moved to seize control of the government. The Paredes administration was teetering on the brink of destruction. On August 3, as a prelude to Santa Anna's return, the garrison at Vera Cruz issued a pronunciamento in favor of Santa Anna, which was echoed by General Salas, the comandante general at Mexico City. From this point on the conclusion was preordained. Justin Smith, *War with Mexico* (New York: Macmillan Co., 1919), 1: 217.

32. The 1st Infantry, consisting of only four companies, was too small to achieve regimental status. Consequently, the Baltimore Battalion, six companies of volunteers from the Washington and Baltimore area, were brigaded with the 1st Infantry to form the ten companies now referred to as the 1st Infantry. John R. Kenly, *Memoirs of a Maryland Volunteer* (Philadelphia: J. B. Lippincott & Co., 1873) 54, 77.

33. John Haskell King joined the 1st Infantry in 1837 at the rank of 2d lieutenant. He was promoted to the rank of captain on October 31, 1846. He rose to the rank of major general in the Union Army and was cited for gallant and meritorious conduct at the battles of Chickamauga and Ruffs Station, Georgia, and for gallant and meritorious service during the war. He died on April 7, 1888. Heitman, *Register,* 1: 599.

34. The steamer *Natchez,* reported by Dilworth as leaving Camargo on August 31, 1846, cannot be traced. There were many charter boats on the Rio Grande during the summer of 1846, and a complete compiled list of steamers that navigated the river does not exist, even to this day. The only boat of that name is reported by Way as a sidewheel packet of 280 tons with a wooden hull, built in Cincinnati, Ohio, in 1846, and owned and commanded by Capt. Thomas P. Leathers. Way, *Directory,* 206.

SEPTEMBER

1. The *Hatchee Eagle* was a sidewheel river steamer of 116 tons built in Louisville, Kentucky, in 1845. She was owned by the United States government and used to transport soldiers and supplies from the

mouth of the Rio Grande to Camargo, Mexico. Kelley, River, 110; Risch, *Quarter Master,* 261.

2. "Get along, Josey" is a Negro version of the song entitled "Jim A-long, Josey" which has as part of the refrain "get a-long, Josey." The song is danced as a Virginia Reel, according to Scarborough's informant, W. R. Boyd, Jr. Dorothy Scarborough, *On the Trail of Negro Folk-Songs* (Cambridge: Harvard University Press, 1925) 104-5.

3. Jacob John Booker graduated from the United States Military Academy in 1843 and was assigned to the 1st Infantry. He died on June 26, 1849. Heitman, *Register,* 1: 230.

4. James G. Soulard Snelling was an 1845 graduate of the United States Military Academy, and assigned to the 8th Infantry. He was cited for gallant and meritorious conduct at the battles of Contreras, Churubusco, and Molino del Rey. He died on August 25, 1855. Heitman, *Register,* 1: 906.

5. The campsite is the village of Guardado Abajo, about nine miles west of Camargo, near the Rio Grande. The village is referred to locally by the shortened first part of the name, pronounced as "wardo."

6. Mier is a small town about thirty miles west of Camargo. It gained fame in the United States as the site of the capture on December 26, 1842, by Mexican forces of the Texans involved in the so-called Mier Expedition. By local reputation, the prettiest ladies in northern Mexico are said to come from this town.

7. Puntiagudo was a small Mexican village located about fifty miles west of Camargo on the main road to Monterrey. The village is remembered by many travelers through this part of the country for its clear running brook, and "near[by] a beautiful cascade, constructed of stone and cement, in order to turn the channel through the town." The town was burned in March 1847 on orders of Col. Samuel Curtis, for alleged guerrilla activities. But the village yet survives, under the new name of "General Treviño."

8. A fandango, probably typical of the ones held in northern Mexico at that time, was attended by Franklin Smith on November 14, 1846, and he wrote these reactions:

> An old Mexican was the fiddler—his only instrument. I was surprised to hear so many tunes familiar to me; among others was Fisher's horn-pipe. The waltz is their greatest dance—they are fondest of it...when they waltzed the Mexican youth generally

> got the show—but few of the voluntarios could go the waltz—the women were dressed principally in silk—with gold beads around the neck. On the N. E. corner of the yard near one of the lights heavy gambling was going on at Monte—at the S. E. corner an old woman had a large table loaded with oranges, pecans & dried figs—I noticed the girls giving back to the old woman the presents of fruits which the vols. gave them—I remarked this & was told that it was a regular perquisite of the old Crone.

Chance, *Mexican War Diary*, 113-14.

9. Lucien Bonaparte Webster graduated from the United States Military Academy in 1823 and was assigned to the 3rd Artillery. He was cited for gallant and meritorious conduct for his actions at the capture of Monterrey and the battle of Buena Vista. Webster died on November 4, 1853. Heitman, *Register*, 1: 1013.

10. William Whann Mackall was a graduate of the United States Military Academy in 1837 and was assigned to the 1st Artillery. He was cited for gallant and meritorious conduct for his actions at the capture of Monterrey, and for his actions in the battles of Contreras and Churubusco. Mackall resigned his commission on July 3, 1861, and rose to the rank of brigadier general in the CSA Army. He died August 19, 1891. Heitman, *Register*, 1: 670.

11. Charles Augustus May joined the 2d Dragoons at the rank of lieutenant in 1836. He was cited for gallant and distinguished service at the battle of Palo Alto, for gallant and highly distinguished service at the battle of Resaca de la Palma, and for gallant and meritorious conduct at the battle of Buena Vista. He rose to the rank of colonel before resigning his commission on April 20, 1861. Heitman, *Register*, 1: 698.

12. Cerralvo is an ancient Mexican town about fifty miles southwest of Camargo along the main line of advance of the American army to Monterrey. During the Mexican War the town claimed about 1,800 citizens. The buildings were mainly of stone with many of the private residences containing formal gardens watered by the many springs of clear, cold water that emerge from the ground south of the town, circulated by a system of canals. B. F. Scribner recorded this wistful remembrance:

> We pitched our tents near the old Spanish town of Cerralvo, which bears the impress of an antiquated fortress, and reminds one of the dilapidated castles we read of in romances. The houses are built of gray stone, with loopholes for windows. Through

> the centre of the town runs a beautiful clear stream spanned by bridges and arches. There is also a cathedral with chimes and a towering steeple. It is said to be 166 years old.

B. F. Scribner, *Camp Life of a Volunteer* (Philadelphia: Grigg, Elliot & Co., 1847), 49.

13. In early 1846, Lt. Col. William S. Harney, stationed at San Antonio with six companies of the 2d Dragoons, led an expedition of troopers and Texan volunteers to the Presidio del Rio Grande. This force was organized and dispatched on Harney's own initiative without the knowledge or approval of the War Department. Harney did not respond promptly to orders for the recall of his command from the Rio Grande, and even considered invading the interior of Mexico as far as Monterrey. He was placed under arrest by his commanding officer, General Wool, and relieved of command when his forces reluctantly returned to San Antonio. L. U. Reavis, *Life of Gen. Wm. S. Harney* (St. Louis: Bryan, Brand & Co., 1878), 154-55.

14. John Ellis Wool joined the service in 1813 at the rank of captain in the 13th Infantry. He served during the Mexican War at the rank of brigadier general. General Wool was cited for gallant conduct in the battle of Plattsburg, September 11, 1814, and for gallant and meritorious conduct at the battle of Buena Vista. He was voted a sword by Congress on January 15, 1854, "That the thanks of Congress are due, and are hereby tendered to Bvt. Maj. Gen. John E. Wool for his distinguished service in the late war with Mexico, and especially for the skill, enterprise, and courage which distinguished his conduct at the battle of Buena Vista; that the President be requested to cause a sword, with suitable devices, to be presented to Gen. Wool." Heitman, *Register,* 1: 1059-60.

15. Charles Ferguson Smith graduated from the United States Military Academy in 1825 and was assigned to the 2d Artillery. He was cited for gallant and distinguished conduct at the battles of Palo Alto and Resaca de la Palma and the capture of Monterrey. He was also cited for his actions at Contreras and Churubusco. He rose to the rank of major general of volunteers in the Union Army and died on April 25, 1862. Heitman, *Register,* 1: 895.

16. The rancho Ramos was about twenty-eight miles northeast of Monterrey and had a population of about 100 persons during the time of the Mexican War. A traveler could acquire there "meat and corn, wood and water." *American Flag,* July 7, 1846.

17. The village of Marin (San Carlos de Marin) is about twenty miles northeast of Monterrey, and at the time of the Mexican War had a population of more than 3,000. Maurice Fulton, *The Diaries and Letters of Josiah Gregg* (Norman: Univ. of Oklahoma Press, 1941), 1: 359; *American Flag*, July 7, 1846.

18. Young 2d Lt. Abner Doubleday, who was on the march to Monterrey with Taylor's forces, recorded his recollections of the events some thirty year later. He remembered

> We saw Mexicans sitting in their doorways along the route to see us pass. They had lost all fear of us, now that they saw we had no intention of injuring peaceful citizens. They said to us "Mucho fandango a Monterey" which is equivalent to they are getting up a dance for you in Monterey.

Doubleday, "Mexican War."

19. Anastacio Torrejón was a Mexican cavalry officer who led a brigade in the attack against the patrol of Seth Thornton at Rancho de Carricitos on April 26, 1846. Torrejón fought at Palo Alto, Resaca de la Palma, Monterrey, and Buena Vista. In central Mexico, he led a brigade at the skirmish at San Gerónimo and in defense of Mexico City. This rather unflattering description of him appeared in the *New Orleans Picayune* of January 28, 1847:

> Torrejon is a mestizo, or half breed, and like most mestizos is by no means distinguished for personal beauty. Like Guerrero and other Mexican officers who have had a large admixture of Indian blood in their veins, Torrejon is very cunning. In laying traps for an adversary he is remarkably expert, and as will be remembered, it was he who surrounded and took prisoners Capt. Thornton's command of forty men.

20. Agua Fría was a rancho about twelve miles northeast of Monterrey. Fulton, *Diary*, 1: 333.

21. While Gen. Taylor had the legal authority to maintain strict control over the regular troops, his legal authority over the volunteer troops was questionable. Volunteer soldiers guilty of crimes not specified in the Military Code of Justice were placed in irons and sent to New Orleans, where they were quickly released. Winfield Scott felt that the politicians in Washington were fearful of the consequences at the ballot box of enacting the legislation necessary to bring civilians under military control. Scott noted:

> Reliable information reached Washington, almost daily that the wild volunteers as soon as beyond the Rio Grande, committed, with impunity, all sorts of atrocities on the persons and properties of Mexicans....There was no legal punishment for any of those offences, for by the strange omission of Congress, American troops take with them beyond the limits of their own country, no law but the Constitution of the United States, and the rules and articles of war. These do not provide any court for the trial or punishment of murder, rape, theft, &c., &c.—no matter by whom or on whom committed.

Scott drew up a paper, titled "Martial Law Order" which a startled William Marcy, Secretary of War, returned to Scott indicating that it was "too explosive for safe handling." Scott sent the paper on to Taylor, advising that it would be left to his own (Taylor's) responsibility as to whether or not it should be adopted. Taylor, evidentally thought the plan too "explosive" also and adopted the policy of placing offenders in irons and sending them home to be tried in New Orleans. Of course, with no witnesses present, the prisoners were quickly released on habeas corpus and never punished for their often heinous crimes against the Mexican people. Winfield Scott, on the other hand, circulated the famous Order No. 20 after his arrival in Mexico, extending the authority of military tribunals over civil crimes, largely on his own authority, without the support of Congress or the president. A few public hangings and floggings quickly restored a peaceful balance between the American military and Mexican civilians. Scott's courageous actions hastened the end of hostilities in Mexico, and are a lasting credit to his brilliant career of service to the nation. Winfield Scott, *Memoirs of Lieutenant-General Scott,* (Freeport: Books for Libraries Press, 1970), 2: 392-94

22. Delos Bennet Sacket graduated from the United States Military Academy in 1845 and was assigned to the 2d Dragoons. He was cited for gallant and meritorious conduct at the battles of Palo Alto and Resaca de la Palma. Sacket rose to the rank of brigadier general and died on March 8, 1885. Heitman, *Register,* 1: 856.

23. The "elephant groan" referred to by Trooper Sackett must have been an idea or phrase spawned from the expression "seen the elephant." The phrase has many meanings, but Bartlett thought that "To see the elephant was to undergo any disappointment of high raised expectations...men who have volunteered for the Mexican war expecting to reap lots of glory and enjoyment, but instead have found only sick-

ness, fatigue, privations, and suffering, are currently said to have 'seen the elephant.' John Russell Bartlett, *Dictionary of Americanisms*, (1848); as quoted from Robert W. Johannsen, *To the Halls of the Montezuma* (New York: Oxford University Press, 1985), 87-90.

24. This camp, located in a grove of walnut trees which were watered by bubbling springs, was a picnic ground known locally as Santo Domingo. The Americans referred to the camp as "Walnut Springs." Several of the American officers slain in the attack on eastern Monterrey were buried in a small cemetery near this camp. This cemetery, perhaps the one in which the remains of Rankin Dilworth were buried, is now lost in the urban sprawl of the modern industrial giant of northern Mexico—Monterrey.

25. William George Williams was an 1824 graduate of the United States Military Academy, and was assigned to the 7th Infantry. He was promoted to the rank of captain in the topological engineers on July 7, 1838. Williams was killed in action on September 21, 1846, during the capture of Monterrey. Heitman, *Register*, 1: 1043.

CONCLUSION

1. Biography of Rankin Dilworth in George W. Cullum, *Biographical Register of the Officers and Graduates of the U. S. Military Academy, From 1802 to 1862* (New York: James Miller, Publisher, 1879), 2: 106.
2. Michael Pilgrim, Military Reference Branch, National Archives, private correspondence of November 16, 1994, to the editors.
3. Capt. W. S. Henry, *Campaign Sketches of the War with Mexico* (New York: Harper & Brothers, 1847), 222.
4. Henry, *Campaign Sketches*, 250. An engraving of the cemetery of the 3d Infantry by Lt. A. Sully, is found on page 251.
5. Henry, *Campaign Sketches*, 249.
6. "Monterrey 20-24 Sept 1846," unpublished notes of Col. Carter L. Hilsabeck, U. S. Army (Ret.), in possession of the editors.

BIBLIOGRAPHY

PRINTED SOURCES

American Flag (Matamoros), 1846-1847.

"An Exploration of a Common Legacy: A Conference on Border Architecture. "*Proceedings*. Texas Historical Commission, 1978.

Barton, Henry W. *Texas Volunteers in the Mexican War.* Wichita Falls, Tex.: Texian Press, 1970.

Bauer, K. Jack. *General Zachary Taylor: Soldier, Planter, Statesman of the Old Southwest.* Baton Rouge: Louisiana State University Press, 1985.

———. *The Mexican War 1846-1848*. New York: Macmillan, 1974.

Bloom, John Porter. *With the American Army into Mexico, 1846-1848*. Ph.D. diss., Emory University, 1956.

Brockett, Oscar G. *History of the Theatre*. Boston: Allyn and Bacon, 1968.

Chance, Joseph E. *Jefferson Davis's Mexican War Regiment.* Jackson: University Press of Mississippi, 1991.

———. *The Mexican War Diary of Captain Franklin Smith.* Jackson: University of Mississippi Press, 1991.

Coker, Caleb. *The News From Brownsville.* Austin: Texas State Historical Assn., 1992.

Conner, J. E. "The Maurice Kavanaugh Simons Diary." MS, Texas A&I University.

Cullum, George W. *Biographical Register of the Officers and Graduates of the U. S. Military Academy, From 1802 to 1867.* New York: James Miller, Pub., 1879.

Curtis, Samuel Ryan. "The Diary of Samuel Ryan Curtis." Bancroft Library, University of California.

Davis, Edward Adams. *The Rivers and Bayous of Louisiana.* Baton Rouge: Louisiana Research Assn., 1968.

Diccionario Porrua Historia, Biografía y Geografía de México. Mexico City: Editorial Porrua, 1965.

Doubleday, Abner. "From the Mexican War to the Rebellion." MS., New York Historical Society.

Duffe, Mary. "Jefferson Barracks." *St. Louis Commerce.* October 1, 1970.

Emory, William H. *Report on the United States Boundary Survey.* Austin: Texas State Historical Assn., 1987.

Ferrell, Robert H., ed. *Monterrey Is Ours! The Mexican War Letters of Lieutenant Dana 1845-1847.* Lexington: University Press of Kentucky, 1990.

Freund, Max. *Gustav Dressel's Houston Journal.* Austin: University of Texas Press, 1954.

Fulton, Maurice. *The Diaries and Letters of Josiah Gregg.* Norman: University of Oklahoma Press, 1941.

Fusco, Tony. "Jefferson Barracks." *St. Louis Commerce.* April 1, 1985.

Ganoe, William A. *The History of the United States Army.* Ashton, Maryland: Eric Lundberg, 1964.

Heitman, Francis B. *Historical Register and Dictionary of the United States Army, From Its Organization, September 29, 1789, to March 2, 1903.* Washington: Government Printing Office, 1903.

Henry, W. S. *Campaign Sketches of The War with Mexico.* New York: Harper & Brothers, 1847.

Johannsen, Robert W. *To the Halls of the Montezuma.* New York: Oxford University Press, 1985.

Johnston, William P. *The Life of Albert Sidney Johnston.* New York: D. Appleton and Co., 1878.

Kane, Harnett T. *Queen New Orleans: City by the River.* New York: Bonanza Books, 1949.

Kearney, Milo and Antony Knopp. *Boom and Bust: The Historical Cycles of Matamoros and Brownsville.* Austin: Eakin Press, 1991.

Kelly, Pat. *River of Lost Dreams.* Lincoln: University of Nebraska Press, 1986.

Kenly, John R. *Memoirs of a Maryland Volunteer.* Philadelphia: J.B. Lippincott and Co., 1873.

Long, E. B. *Personal Memoirs of U.S. Grant.* Cleveland: World Publishing Co., 1952.

Lytle, William and Forrest R. Holdcamper. *Merchant Steam Vessels of the United States: 1790-1868.* Staten Island, N.Y.: Steamship Historical Society of America, 1975.

McEniry, Sister Blanche Marie. *American Catholics in the War with Mexico.* Washington: Catholic Universiy, 1932.

McIntosh, James T. *The Papers of Jefferson Davis.* Baton Rouge: Louisiana State University Press, 1974.

Matlof, Maurice, ed. *American Military History.* Rev. ed. Washington D.C.: Office of the Chief of Military History, 1973.

Meade, George Gordon. *The Life and Letters of George Gordon Meade.* New York: Charles Scriber's Sons, 1913.

Monroe, Haskell M., Jr., and James T. McIntosh. *The Papers of Jefferson Davis.* Baton Rouge: Louisiana State University Press, 1971.

Myers, William Starr. *The Mexican War Diary of George B. McCellan.* Princeton, N.J.: Princeton University Press, 1917.

Nevins, Allan. *Polk: The Diary of a President.* London: Longmans, Green and Co., 1952.

Parker, Captain William Harwar. *Recollections of a Naval Officer: 1841-1865.* New York: Charles Scribner's Sons, 1885.

Reavis, L. U. *Life of General William S. Harney.* St. Louis: Bryan, Brand & Co., 1878.

Reid, Samuel. *The Scouting Expeditions of McCulloch's Rangers.* Austin: Steck Co., 1935.

Reilly, Thomas William. "American Reporters and the Mexican War." Ph.D. diss., University of Minnesota, 1975.

Register of Graduates and Former Cadets-1802-1980-U.S.M.A. West Point: Assn. of Graduates, USMA, 1980.

Risch, Erna. *Quarter Master Support of the Army: A History of the Corps: 1775-1939.* Washington: Office of the Quarter Master General, 1962.

Ripley, R. S. *The War with Mexico.* New York: Burt Franklin, 1970.

Robinson, John B. *Reminiscences of a Campaign in Mexico, by a Member of the "Bloody First"* Nashville: John York & Co., 1849.

Scarborough, Dorothy. *On the Trail of Negro Folk-Songs.* Cambridge: Harvard University Press, 1925.

Schult, Joachim. *The Sailing Dictionary: A Comprehensive Reference Book of Modern Sailing Terms.* Frogmore, St. Albans: Granada Publishing Co., 1981.

Scott, Winfield. *Memoirs of Lieutenant General Scott.* Freeport, N. Y.: Books for Libraries Press, 1970.

Scribner, B. F. *Camp Life of a Volunteer.* Philadelphia: Grigg, Elliot and Co., 1847.

Silver, James W. *Edmund Pendleton Gaines, Frontier General.* Baton Rouge: Louisiana State University Press, 1949.

Singletary, Otis A. *The Mexican War.* Chicago: University of Chicago Press, 1960.

Smith, Justin Harvey. *The War with Mexico.* 2 vols. New York: Macmillan Co., 1919.

Spurlin, Charles D. *Texas Veterans in the Mexican War.* Nacogdoches, Tex.: Erickson Press, 1984.

Viele, Teresa Griffin. *Following the Drum: A Glimpse of Frontier Life.* Lincoln: University of Nebraska Press, 1984.

Way, Fred, Jr. *Way's Packet Directory: 1848-1983.* Athens: Ohio University Press, 1983.

Webb, Walter Prescott, ed. *The Handbook of Texas.* 2 vols. Austin: Texas State Historical Assn., 1952.

———. *The Texas Rangers.* Austin: University of Texas Press, 1935.

INTERVIEW

Passel, Charles. Interview by Lawrence Clayton, November 18, 1991.

OTHER SOURCES

ORDERS

General Orders, vol. 43. Justin Smith Papers, University of Texas Library, Austin.

Order 101, Orders of General Zachary Taylor to the Army of Occupation in the Mexican War, National Archive and Records Service.

Order 103, Orders of General Zachary Taylor to the Army of Occupation in the Mexican War, National Archive and Records Service.

Justin Smith Transcripts, Latin American Collection, University of Texas at Austin, Austin, Texas.

Private unpublished notes of Col. Carter L. Hilsabeck in possession of the editors.

LETTERS

Rankin Dilworth to J. P. Poinsett, April 20, 1840.

Michael E. Pilgrim to Joseph E. Chance, November 16, 1994.